MI DAILY DEVOTION

(Second Edition)

100 days of God's promises, God's provision, God's protection,
practical Christian living, personal experiences, God's power,
peace with God and peace in God.

ELY ROQUE SAGANSAY

WestBow
PRESS
A DIVISION OF THOMAS NELSON

Scripture taken from the King James Version of the Bible.

Edited by: Eliel Lyn Dumala Sagansay and Ely Roque Sagansay
Photo: Ely R. Sagansay

WestBow Press books may be ordered through booksellers or by contacting:

WestBow Press
A Division of Thomas Nelson
1663 Liberty Drive
Bloomington, IN 47403
www.westbowpress.com
1-(866) 928-1240

ISBN: 978-1-4497-6733-4 (sc)
ISBN: 978-1-4497-6735-8 (hc)
ISBN: 978-1-4497-6734-1 (e)

Library of Congress Control Number: 2012917549

Printed in the United States of America

WestBow Press rev. date: 10/03/2012

FOREWORD

Time... is what everyone is hoping they could have more of. The common question everyone may ask is: "If I could only have more time with my family, with my friends, with my job and most especially with God...?" Pastor Ely Sagansay's second edition of MI DAILY DEVOTION gives us that almost rare and precious commodity these days called "time with God". It is rich, both with the abundance of God's Word and also with the writer's honest and personal experiences in life and ministry. As a Pastor, I once heard someone said like this, "We should not only learn from our own experiences, we should also learn from the experiences of others." I thank the Lord for Pastor Ely's desire to help us spend more time with our Master!

Rev. Dr. Dennis V. Casaje, OD, DMin
Pastor, Wilshire Baptist Church
Los Angeles, CA

DEDICATION

To my wife: Bermilin Dumala Sagansay and my children; Eliezer,
Ely (JR), Eliel Lyn and Elmer John (EJ)
To my church: International Community Christian Church –
Trenton, Michigan.
To my dear friend and partner in the ministry; Reverend Jimmy
Jones and his church- First Baptist Church of Trenton, Michigan.

SUNDAY

ACCEPTING GOD'S FREE GIFT OF SALVATION

(John 1:12) "But as many as received him, to them gave he power to become the sons of God, even to them that believe on his name:"

Accept that you are a sinner before God. "10- As it is written, There is none righteous, no, not one:" 23- "For all have sinned, and come short of the glory of God;" (Romans 3:10, 23) I know it would not be easy to humbly come in the presence of God and to ask for forgiveness of our sins. It means that you also have to accept your depravity and your need for the blood of Christ to wash you and cleanse you of your sins. "In whom we have redemption through his blood, the forgiveness of sins, according to the riches of his grace;" (Ephesians 1:7)

Believe and accept Christ as your Lord and Savior. When you accept Christ as your Lord and Savior; it means you will also accept His Lordship, His shed blood, His finished work at the cross of Calvary. You also accept Him as the second person of the holy trinity. You heard of people say that; "Christians made it so easy to go to heaven". Actually it was not the Christians who made it easy, it was the work of the holy trinity through the death of the Lord Jesus Christ on the cross. Because of what He has done at the cross, all we have to do is to accept it by faith. Accept the free gift of salvation. The gift was offered, but the question is; would you be willing to accept that gift by humbly coming to God and accepting such gift by faith? "23- For the wages of sin is death; but the gift of God is eternal life through Jesus Christ our Lord." 16- "For God so loved the world, that he gave his only begotten Son, that whosoever believeth in him should not perish, but have everlasting life." (Romans 6:23; John 3:16)

Confess your sins to God "7- But if we walk in the light, as he is in the light, we have fellowship one with another, and the blood of Jesus Christ his Son cleanseth us from all sin. 8- If we say that we have no sin, we deceive ourselves, and the truth is not in us. 9- If we confess our sins, he is faithful and just to forgive us our sins, and to cleanse us from all unrighteousness. 10- If we say that we have not sinned, we make him a liar, and his word is not in us." (I John 1:7- 10) Someone said; "To confess, it means to say it, to look at it and deal with it as it is." You don't confess your sins to an individual or religious leader. You confess your sins to God because we have sinned and offended Him. When you confess your sins to God; it means you admit your sinfulness and your marred spiritual condition. Charles H. Spurgeon wrote; "It may be that you are unsaved. Why? Do you think the plan of salvation laid down in our text is untrue? How can that be, when God has pledged His own word? Do you think it is too easy? Why then are not saved?" (Morning and Evening- October 05, Evening) The Bible says; "1- In those days came John the Baptist, preaching in the wilderness of Judaea, 2- And saying, Repent ye: for the kingdom of heaven is at hand." (Matthew 3:1- 2)

MONDAY
START SERVING THE LORD

(Acts 20:19- 21) "19- Serving the Lord with all humility of mind, and with many tears, and temptations, which befell me by the lying in wait of the Jews: 20- And how I kept back nothing that was profitable unto you, but have showed you, and have taught you publicly, and from house to house, 21- Testifying both to the Jews, and also to the Greeks, repentance toward God, and faith toward our Lord Jesus Christ."

Don't let yourself be comfortable seating in a dead church or a church where you can't even feel the presence and glory of God. Churches have lost its passion, and they don't use its full potential or failed to exercise their faith and privileges as God's children which is to serve the King of kings.

Here are some of the benefits in serving the Lord "And ye shall serve the LORD your God, and he shall bless thy bread, and thy water; and I will take sickness away from the midst of thee." (Exodus 23:25) "And now, Israel, what doth the LORD thy God require of thee, but to fear the LORD thy God, to walk in all his ways, and to love him, and to serve the LORD thy God with all thy heart and with all thy soul," (Deuteronomy 10:12) Serving God is not an option for Christians; it is our duty to do our best for God. We can have blessings from the Lord as we serve Him faithfully. The Bible says; "We should walk after the LORD our God, and fear him, and keep his commandments, and obey his voice, and we shall serve him, and cleave unto him." "...yet turn not aside from following the LORD, but serve the LORD with all your heart;" (I Samuel 12:20) "Now therefore fear the LORD, and serve him in sincerity and in truth: and put away the gods which your fathers served on the other side of the flood, and in Egypt; and serve ye the LORD." (Joshua 24:14) Notice what Apostle Paul reminded the Christians during his times and it's the same message for us Christians of this present time. When I was a little boy in a small church in Bacolod city, Philippines where I grew up in a Sunday school; I remember a beautiful godly family that made a difference in my life. There was a man in that small church who was commonly known as Manoy Abe. He was a family centered man. He loves the Lord and he served the Lord with his family in a small Baptist church in our province. He was a Christian who put (Joshua 24:15) into practiced and made it his lifestyle. In verse 15- "And if it seem evil unto you to serve the LORD, choose you this day whom ye will serve; whether the gods which your fathers served that were on the other side of the flood, or the gods of the Amorites, in whose land ye dwell: but as for me and my house, we will serve the LORD." Apostle Paul said; "19- What? Know ye not that your body is the temple of the Holy Ghost which is in you, which ye have of God, and ye are not your own? 20- For ye are bought with a price: therefore glorify God in your body, and in your spirit, which are God's." (I Corinthians 6:19- 20)

TUESDAY
PERSEVERE UNTIL YOU REACH YOUR GOALS

(Hebrews 12:1- 3) "1- Wherefore seeing we also are compassed about with so great a cloud of witnesses, let us lay aside every weight, and the sin which doth so easily beset us, and let us run with patience the race that is set before us, 2- Looking unto Jesus the author and finisher of our faith; who for the joy that was set before him endured the cross, despising the shame, and is set down at the right hand of the throne of God. 3- For consider him that endured such contradiction of sinners against himself, lest ye be wearied and faint in your minds."

According to Webster's Dictionary: "Persevere" means – "to persist in anything undertaken", "Maintain a purpose in spite of difficulty, obstacles, or discouragement", "Continue steadfastly."

Pray earnestly and plan wisely as you set your goals. We have daily goals, weekly goals, monthly goals and yearly goals; but we must have long ranged goals as well. Apostle Paul wrote; "12- Not as though I had already attained, either were already perfect: but I follow after, if that I may apprehend that for which also I am apprehended of Christ Jesus. 13- Brethren, I count not myself to have apprehended: but this one thing I do, forgetting those things which are behind, and reaching forth unto those things which are before, 14- I press toward the mark for the prize of the high calling of God in Christ Jesus." (Philippians 3:12- 14)

Entrust your goals to God knowing that we can't do anything without Him. "I am the vine, ye are the branches: He that abideth in me, and I in him, the same bringeth forth much fruit: for without me ye can do nothing."; "I can do all things through Christ which strengtheneth me." (John 15:5; Philippians 4:13)

Re-Set your goals if you failed, but don't quit. You may have just started to walk through the aisle of the learning process. You're not a loser as long as you keep on keeping on! Burn that bridges named: "quit" or "looking back". Those were the failures of the Israelites when they went out of Egypt. Mr. Edison said; "Many of life's failures are people who did not realize how close they were to success when they gave up." "I have not failed. I've just found 10,000 ways that won't work." Thomas Edison 1847-1931

The Bible says; "24- Know ye not that they which run in a race run all, but one receiveth the prize? So run, that ye may obtain. 25- And every man that striveth for the mastery is temperate in all things. Now they do it to obtain a corruptible crown; but we an incorruptible. 26- I therefore so run, not as uncertainly; so fight I, not as one that beateth the air: 27- But I keep under my body, and bring it into subjection: lest that by any means, when I have preached to others, I myself should be a castaway." (I Corinthians 9:24- 27)

Start working hard and wisely to get to your goals. Don't take things lightly and don't let laziness gets in the way. "He also that is slothful in his work is brother to him that is a great waster." 24- "A slothful man hideth his hand in his bosom, and will not so much as bring it to his mouth again."; "Not slothful in business; fervent in spirit; serving the Lord;" (Romans 12:11; Proverbs 18:9; 19:24)

Exercise caution and exert more efforts as you work hard. Jesus said, "…be wise as serpent and harmless as dove."

Visualize your way to success. When you reach your goals, celebrate success for God and with God. Paul gave the glory back to God and he honored the Lord in his victory. Paul said; "57- But thanks be to God, which giveth us the victory through our Lord Jesus Christ. 58- Therefore, my beloved brethren, be ye stedfast, unmoveable, always abounding in the work of the Lord, forasmuch as ye know that your labour is not in vain in the Lord." (I Corinthians 15:57- 58)

Entertain good advice and counsels. "14- Where no counsel is, the people fall: but in the multitude of counsellors there is safety." 22- Without counsel purposes are disappointed: but in the multitude of counsellors they are established." (Proverbs 11:14; 15:22)

Review your failures or successes and examine yourself. "2- Examine me, O LORD, and prove me; try my reins and my heart." 5- "Examine yourselves, whether ye be in the faith; prove your own selves. Know ye not your own selves, how that Jesus Christ is in you, except ye be reprobates?" (Psalm 26:2; II Corinthians 13:5)

Evaluate where you are in all areas of life. Your success in reaching your goals in spiritual, financial and physical standing in life will depend on your relationship with the Lord and your attitude towards life, towards your family and others.

P-e-r-s-e-v-e-r-e until you reach your goals and have your dream comes true... "24- Know ye not that they which run in a race run all, but one receiveth the prize? So run, that ye may obtain. 25- And every man that striveth for the mastery is temperate in all things. Now they do it to obtain a corruptible crown; but we an incorruptible." (I Corinthians 9:24- 25)

WEDNESDAY
MANAGE YOUR TIME, TALENTS AND TREASURES WISELY

(Proverbs 25:13) "As the cold of snow in the time of harvest, so is a faithful messenger to them that send him: for he refresheth the soul of his masters."

Have you ever wondered how much time, talents and treasures are being wasted every day? If the Philippines have 91,983,000 in population and according to July 2009 census; the Philippines has 7.6% unemployment rate. It means you are talking of about more or less 6,990,708 of jobless people of which most of them could be bystanders and they're not doing anything. If each of them would loss 60 minutes each day; it would be 1,440 minutes in 24 hours for doing nothing, and just imagine how much time are being lost and were spent for nothing. It would approximately be about 419,442,480 for all of them. I can't just imagine the wasted times and wasted opportunities people have missed. There are people in some parts of the world who are idle for hours or days. Wasted times and days!

There are those who have all the talents in the world, but they just don't know how to get to their destination. They don't know how to reach those goals. No one motivates them to pursue their dreams and ambitions. No one gave them the opportunity or at least gave them a try. There were no challenges and opportunities for them. They don't have the guts to step up into the next level. They've wasted their talents because no one opens the door for them or at least show an interest. They have talents but they have no clue and may be they don't know how to manage their talents and their time. Some young people and church members their talents got confined in a box; their own box. Some are just afraid to step up or step out of their box. One of the ministries of music prescription is to develop talents, because Eliezer my son know what it means to be alone out there.

We need more Jabez's of this present time. He made something significant in spite of his background and personal weaknesses. "9- And Jabez was more honourable than his brethren: and his mother called his name Jabez, saying, because I bare him with sorrow. 10- And Jabez called on the God of Israel, saying, Oh that thou wouldest bless me indeed, and enlarge my coast, and that thine hand might be with me, and that thou wouldest keep me from evil, that it may not grieve me! And God granted him that which he requested." (I Chronicles 4:9- 10)

How about your treasures? *What are your treasures?* The question could be *who are your treasures?* Do you manage your treasures according to God's perspective, according to God's will for us and according to His Word? We cannot afford to waste another time, talent and treasure while we are here on earth living for our Jesus. Sometimes, if I looked back from my younger years and would think of how much time and resources I've wasted as a youth; I get disappointed and I felt bad for myself although I know it's wrong to live in the past. But it happens every day, every hour and every minute. Young people are not just wasting their time but talents and resources. I believe that every Christian should know, memorize and live these verses about what Jesus said in the Bible; "19- Lay not up for yourselves treasures upon earth, where moth and rust doth corrupt, and where thieves break through and steal: 20- But lay up for yourselves treasures in heaven, where neither moth nor rust doth corrupt, and where thieves do not break through nor steal: 21- For where your treasure is, there will your heart be also." (Matthew 6:19- 21)

THURSDAY

THINGS TO BE THANKFUL TO GOD FOR...

(Psalm 100:4) "Enter into his gates with thanksgiving, and into his courts with praise: be thankful unto him, and bless his name."

(II Corinthians 9:15) "Thanks be unto God for his unspeakable gift." (Psalms 30:12) "To the end that my glory may sing praise to thee, and not be silent. O LORD my God, I will give thanks unto thee forever."

We must give thanks to God: 1- Give thanks to God for His unspeakable gifts. 2- Let's be thankful to God for the salvation that God gave us through our Lord Jesus Christ. 3- We can also rejoice and be grateful for the spiritual blessings that He blessed us with. 4- And we can also look forward to the heavenly places which God prepared for those who come to Him in humility of spirit. Paul said that we have His grace and the Lord made us accepted in the beloved. One of the things that we may take for granted is *"the redemption through his blood"*. It was not of money, blood of the animals or of man's way, man's will or man-made salvation; but through His blood. 5- We can also look up to God with gratefulness for the forgiveness of our sins through Jesus Christ. The guilt, the dirty conscience and burdens are all gone, because we were forgiven. 6- Thank God for the brethren and pray for them. Keep them in your prayers and be thankful to God for the wisdom and knowledge from above. 7- I'm so thankful to God for being a part of your life by sharing to you the Lord's unspeakable gift and spiritual blessings through His Words of wisdom. Today, don't hesitate to say, "Thank you...".

One day while I was walking down to my room in Ramada hotel few hours before our "Ramada Worship Night"; behind me was a group of sports team who visited Taylor, Michigan for a game. I was not nosey in their conversations, but I overheard the remarks of 1 of the kids. He said; "I hate this hotel, I hate this place and I don't want to stay in this place!" If you are in a carpeted hotel, with swimming pool, gym, spa and game room, television with cable and internet, how can you hate such place? I would not be surprise on the attitudes of some of the children who don't know what it means to be poor, who don't know anything about poverty, who've never seen people living in shanties or living with nothing but pillows and roof. Have you ever thank the Lord for the freedom that we have in Him? We can also be so grateful for the freedom of this great nation that we have. You can go to bed and get up in the morning and not be worried of the oppression, political and religious persecution from the government. We have witnessed the violence and the riots in some parts of the world. We have turmoil, tribulation and tension on every side. We should be thankful to God for the peace of mind in spite of what's going on in our world today. We have His love and the comfort of the Holy Spirit. My niece prayed over the meal and said; "God is good and God is great, I thank you Lord for the food we eat. Amen" You may have heard of the funny prayers of the little kids like this one, but they're serious about their prayers. One of the girl prayed; "Lord thank you because mom and dad did not fight today." Or "Lord, I thank you for uncle who can afford to buy us a television and we don't have to pray to you and trust you for it…" I believe they really mean it.

Notice Paul's comforting words; "Blessed be the God and Father of our Lord Jesus Christ, who hath blessed us with all spiritual blessings in heavenly places in Christ:" (Ephesians 2: 3)

FRIDAY
GOD'S WAY

(Deuteronomy 6:6- 7) "6- And these words, which I command thee this day, shall be in thine heart: 7- And thou shalt teach them diligently unto thy children, and shalt talk of them when thou sittest in thine house, and when thou walkest by the way, and when thou liest down, and when thou risest up."

I've shared this part of the message and illustration in the other portion of our devotional, but I'm sharing this again for the sake of the message about God's way… I've been thinking about this for a long time. If God wants you to spend 5 minutes of your time 10 years before you die; where would you spend it? Would you spend that 5 minutes at the feet of Jesus in holy ground or in hell with Satan and his angels? Or would you spend it with those who are in hell, with those who rejected the salvation offered to us by God?

Here are some of the reasons why 5 minutes of your time might be important in your life 5 or 10 years before your death:

- So you could make used of your time wisely and for the glory of God.
- You will be more passionate for God and the lost world.
- You will love God and your families.
- You will read and love your Bible every day and you spend more time in prayer.
- You will have the boldness to witness and walk by faith and be a better Christian.

But do we need to spend 5 minutes of our time before the throne of God? And do we need to spend 5 minutes of our time in hell with Satan and his angels or with the lost in hell? I don't think so. What we need is the Holy Spirit of God to enlighten us and make us see our sinfulness and see God's holiness and the needs of the lost world. They need our Savior more than anything this sinful world can offer. Remember one of the songs of the Beatles: "All you need is love…" True indeed; all you need is the love of God. C.S. Lewis wrote; "The Christian does not think God will love us because we are good, but that God will make us good because He loves us." (Goodreads.com – quotes about religion)

I believe that if each one of us will have this single word called "*love*"; our world would have been a better place to live in. There will be *peace* at home, in the palace, at work and even in the tribes and in the mountains where there are tribal conflicts. The Bible said; "For God so loved the world, that he gave his only begotten Son, that whosoever believeth in him should not perish, but have everlasting life." (John 3:16)

Christians must remember that not only that we need the love of God; we also need the love for God. "28- And one of the scribes came, and having heard them reasoning together, and perceiving that he had answered them well, asked him, Which is the first commandment of all? 29- And Jesus answered him, The first of all the commandments is, Hear, O Israel; The Lord our God is one Lord: 30- And thou shalt love the Lord thy God with all thy heart, and with all thy soul, and with all thy mind, and with all thy strength: this is the first commandment. 31- And the second is like, namely this, Thou shalt love thy neighbour as thyself. There is none other commandment greater than these." (Mark 12: 28- 31)

SATURDAY

MOMS AND WIVES; YOU MUST HAVE THE "4 P's"

(I Peter 3:1- 2) "1- Likewise, ye wives, be in subjection to your own husbands; that, if any obey not the word, they also may without the word be won by the conversation of the wives; 2- While they behold your chaste conversation coupled with fear."

If you're a husband you will love to see your wife having these 4 "P's" which I believe would be the desire of every husband. And your desire is for your relationship with your spouse to be closer, happier and stronger as the days go by.

PURE- "4- But let it be the hidden man of the heart, in that which is not corruptible, even the ornament of a meek and quiet spirit, which is in the sight of God of great price. 5- For after this manner in the old time the holy women also, who trusted in God, adorned themselves, being in subjection unto their own husbands:" (I Peter 3: 4- 5) Do we have that hidden man of the heart? Whatever we have in our hearts will manifest in our outside appearances. People only see the outside part of your body, but God sees the heart. Whether you are single or married; stay pure in the sight of God and man.

PERFECT- What do I mean of perfect? Does it mean that you have to be perfect as a mother or a wife like you will never commit any sin or make any mistake? In theology we call it "sinless perfection". Only the holy trinity and the angels in heaven are sinless. (I Peter 5: 10) "But the God of all grace, who hath called us unto his eternal glory by Christ Jesus, after that ye have suffered a while, make you perfect, stablish, strengthen, settle you." It means you must grow spiritually and we must grow in His grace and in the knowledge of the Lord Jesus Christ. Christians have witnessed how God have worked in us and through us and how He made us grow or mature in His grace after we went through sufferings.

PRODUCTIVE- How would you know if a woman, a mother or your wife is really productive? Is there a certain level of spirituality? How would you know if you're productive as a wife or a mother? How can you gauge yourself? Is there any area in our lives as a married man or woman that could tell our effectiveness and productivity? It would be a great treasure for a husband and children as well to see their mother as a productive Sunday school teacher, house wife or church secretary. We need godly parents who loves the Lord and productive at home and in the ministry. You will see the picture of a productive mother according to (Proverbs 31:10- 31)

POSITIVE- Sometimes it's the dad that is so negative but there are wives that are so negative too. It's probably annoying for some to work with negative people. Even in their blessings and answered prayers; some still question God with such blessings and answered prayers. Read and study the scenario in the book of (Acts 12: 11- 16) and in (Proverbs 31: 29- 31). We need good, positive, mature and pure mothers and wives. We seldom see excellent mothers in this present generation.

SUNDAY

WATCH AND PRAY- JESUS IS COMING SOON!

(I Timothy 4:5) "But watch thou in all things, endure afflictions, do the work of an evangelist, make full proof of thy ministry."

"Be ready, Jesus is coming soon!" Those are the words that I heard from an Indian man (a preacher from India) with a brief case in his hand and on its brief case is a sticker with the message: "Be ready, Jesus is coming soon" He was preaching the same phrase over and over in Bacolod Plaza, Philippines. I was just a little boy when I first met this guy. I met him the second time in front of the night club where I used to work in Manila before I came to know the Lord. I was about between 20 to 22 years old when I met him again with the same style of preaching, the same briefcase and the same message: *"Be ready, Jesus is coming soon!"* This message really hit me and hunted my mind and conscience which caused me to really be afraid of what would happen to me if Jesus will come? Will I make it to heaven and be with Jesus?

The Bible said: "But watch thou in all things, endure afflictions, do the work of an evangelist, make full proof of thy ministry." There is a literal Jesus who is coming. "Watch, therefore, for ye know not what hour your Lord doth come." (Matthew 24:42)

I have a kid's song that I wrote few years ago that goes like this:

"Jesus is coming soon, you must be ready, I don't know
when, May be today,
In John 14:1 to 3, Jesus has promised me He has prepared a
place for me.
The Lord Jehovah, Our Blessed Savior, Who reigns in Glory,
We must be ready. When Jesus comes we have no time to
count from 1 to 3,
When Jesus comes, we have no time to read from A to Z,
The Christians will fly, up, up in the sky, Hallelujah in the
twinkling of an eye.
Jesus is coming soon, I'm always ready, I don't know when,

May be today, First John chapter 3 verse two, Jesus has
promised me,
When He comes again, I will be like Him."

What a beautiful song to ponder upon on the coming of the Lord
Jesus Christ. One day God will say the same thing about what he said
to Noah during the flood. And it would be when God will destroy
the whole earth after the tribulation, in His judgment. In (Genesis
8:1) "And God remembered Noah, and every living thing, and all
the cattle that was with him in the ark: and God made a wind to pass
over the earth, and the waters asswaged;" But in (Genesis 7:23- 24)
here in these verses; it tells us of God's righteous wrath and how
God extinguished the whole mankind except Noah and his family.
But the Bible said, "And God remembered Noah, and every living
thing..." "26- And then shall they see the Son of man coming in the
clouds, with great power and glory." "13-Looking for that blessed
hope, and the glorious appearing of the great God and our Savior,
Jesus Christ." (Mark 13:26; Titus 2:13)

MONDAY

THE RAPTURE OF THE CHURCH

(I Thessalonians 4: 14- 18) "14- For if we believe that Jesus died and rose again, even so them also which sleep in Jesus will God bring with him. 15- For this we say unto you by the word of the Lord, that we which are alive and remain unto the coming of the Lord shall not prevent them which are asleep. 16- For the Lord himself shall descend from heaven with a shout, with the voice of the archangel, and with the trump of God: and the dead in Christ shall rise first: 17- Then we which are alive and remain shall be caught up together with them in the clouds, to meet the Lord in the air: and so shall we ever be with the Lord. 18- Wherefore comfort one another with these words."

In the Philippines; some of the people in that beautiful country are following some religious groups and leaders who claimed to be the Christ or the Messiah. They have what they called the "Tatang" or "father" who claims that he was sent by God the Father to be the Messiah and he claims that he is the coming Messiah as prophesied in the Bible. A religious group in the Philippines called Iglesia ni cristo (church of christ) claims that Felix Manalo is higher and greater than Jesus. And we are not just talking about the Philippines, but all over the world.

The world system and its structure will change and the leadership will change, but the Word of the Lord will stay the same. God will still be God. We have observed how our world has changed. The technology and the means of communications have changed. Years ago the Philippines has a very poor communication systems. Now the Philippines were named the text center or text capital of the world. The industry or business dealings have changed. Now we have ebay and internet stores. Everything may change in just a matter of time; but what the Bible said about the coming prophecies will never change. Actually, everything that's going on in the world has something to do with the second coming of Christ.

We must understand that there are 2 phases of the second coming of Christ. The first is the *RAPTURE* of the church and the second phase is the *SECOND COMING of CHRIST* where He will reign for a thousand years. I hope and pray that we are all ready for the coming of our Lord and Savior Jesus Christ. Let's keep ourselves busy for the work of the Lord, because we have but a very short time. Let's work hard and get the Lord's business of reaching the lost be on the top priority; because *"Jesus is coming soon"*. It's good to be an accomplished person, but I don't think it would be better than the Lord's coming. Let us look forward to the second coming of Christ and the marriage of the Lamb.

"23- Then if any man shall say unto you, Lo, here is Christ, or there; believe it not. 24- For there shall arise false Christs, and false prophets, and shall show great signs and wonders; insomuch that, if it were possible, they shall deceive the very elect. 27- For as the lightning cometh out of the east, and shineth even unto the west; so shall also the coming of the Son of man be. 30- And then shall appear the sign of the Son of man in heaven: and then shall all the tribes of the earth mourn, and they shall see the Son of man coming in the clouds of heaven with power and great glory." (Matthew 24: 23 –24; 27; 30)

TUESDAY
WHO WANTS SUCCESS ANYWAYS?

(Joshua 1:8 -9) "8- This book of the law shall not depart out of thy mouth; but thou shalt meditate therein day and night, that thou mayest observe to do according to all that is written therein: for then thou shalt make thy way prosperous, and then thou shalt have good success. 9- Have not I commanded thee? Be strong and of a good courage; be not afraid, neither be thou dismayed: for the LORD thy God is with thee whithersoever thou goest."

It is very obvious that (Joshua 1:1- 9) was talking about the promised of success and prosperity. We have here:

1- *The Consistency of the Instructions.* God was consistent in His command to the Israelites.
2- *The Clarity of the Instructions.* God made it clear to Joshua and He gave them a very clear instructions.
3- *The Continuity of the Instructions.* God have the same instructions to every believer all over the world and to every generation. "Be strong and of a good courage..." And we must read, meditate and live the Word of God.

According to Webster's Dictionary; *"success" means- "Favorable result; Good fortune, Prosperity; Something that succeeds." People may think of success if you're:*

- *Bill Gates, Donald Trump, or Warren Buffet*; It means you're *wealthy.* They have *financial power* and they're very successful. People may think that way; but they are also a needy people no matter how much money they have in the bank. "Because thou sayest, I am rich, and increased with goods, and have need of nothing; and knowest not that thou art wretched, and miserable, and poor, and blind, and naked:" (Revelation 3:17)

- *The celebrities,* It means success to them is being *famous.* They have lost their freedom and privacy. A dear friend of mine said to me about those who are famous, he said; "Ely, the famous, they don't have the freedom to go to the thrift store and carnivals."

- *The politicians–* It means you are *influential and with political power.* It's just so easy to look up to people with so much influence and power, especially political power. But they too have their own struggles and personal weaknesses and problems. It may seem that they have the whole world in their hands; but they may have more worries and problems than you do. No wonder we have some corrupt politicians who are worried of losing their position and constituents. So they take bribe and they bribed.

- *Your next door neighbors, your friends or people you know who gets to travel around the world.* I've known people and friends who visited almost every part of the world, but they're not happy. Some of them are struggling with something and with life itself. Others are struggling with debts.

- *You're a respected individual.* I know of highly intellectual people who were treated like uneducated individuals; because of their mistakes, failures and bad attitude. Some have lost their integrity because of sin and immorality. *Respect can be gained in a process of time, if you are living a life with integrity and dignity.* (II Timothy 4:7- 8). According to John C. Maxwell, "Success is choosing to enter the arena of action, determined to give yourself to the cause that will better humanity and last for eternity." For me; "Success is living happily with your families, serving the Lord and using your potential in full capacity for His Name and for His glory"

WEDNESDAY
THE PROBLEMS OF THE DISCIPLES

(Mark 11: 23- 26) "23- For verily I say unto you, That whosoever shall say unto this mountain, Be thou removed, and be thou cast into the sea; and shall not doubt in his heart, but shall believe that those things which he saith shall come to pass; he shall have whatsoever he saith. 24- Therefore I say unto you, What things soever ye desire, when ye pray, believe that ye receive them, and ye shall have them. 25- And when ye stand praying, forgive, if ye have ought against any: that your Father also which is in heaven may forgive you your trespasses. 26- But if ye do not forgive, neither will your Father which is in heaven forgive your trespasses. Here are some of the problems of the disciples and could be your problems too:

- **Mountain**, verse *"23- For verily I say unto you, That whosoever shall say unto this mountain, Be thou removed,"* We are the Lord's disciples and we have our own mountain. Your mountain could be a thing, a person or your uncontrolled circumstances, your discouragement and depression. You may be coming down from a mountain top experienced and you've just conquered that mountain of problems and trials.

- **Doubt**, 23- *"… and shall not doubt in his heart, but shall believe that those things which he saith shall come to pass; he shall have whatsoever he saith."* We doubt God, we doubt His Word, we doubt His love, we doubt His power and we have our enemy before us which is the devil.

- **"Trespasses and Forgiveness…"** is one of their problems in verse, 25 and (Luke 17: 3-5) "Take heed to yourselves: If thy brother trespass against thee, rebuke him; and if he repent, forgive him. 4- And if he trespass against thee seven times in a day, and seven times in a day turn again to thee, saying, I repent; thou shalt forgive him."

Forgiveness means forgetting the sin, mistakes, fault of the other party without any condition or resentment. Forgiveness is dropping off all your baggage behind you in the ocean of love- the love of God, and not to be taken back forever and ever.

I was watching INVICTUS on a DVD and I was touched and amazed how Mr. Nelson Mandela forgave his political opponents and all those who helped put him in prison and made his life miserable. The way I observed and imagine his life in prison for more than 25 years is something that's really hard for an individual to say; "Come and join my team because you're forgiven." I recommend this movie to everyone who may be struggling with forgiveness.

Take the advice of John in (I John 5: 7- 9) "7- But if we walk in the light, as he is in the light, we have fellowship one with another, and the blood of Jesus Christ his Son cleanseth us from all sin. 8- If we say that we have no sin, we deceive ourselves, and the truth is not in us. 9- If we confess our sins, he is faithful and just to forgive us our sins, and to cleanse us from all unrighteousness."

THURSDAY
THE PROMISES FOR THE DISCIPLES

(Luke 24:49; Acts 1:4) "49- And, behold, I send the promise of my Father upon you: but tarry ye in the city of Jerusalem, until ye be endued with power from on high." "4- And, being assembled together with them, commanded them that they should not depart from Jerusalem, but wait for the promise of the Father, which, saith he, ye have heard of me."

According to Dictionary.com, *promise* means: "an undertaking or assurance given by one person to another agreeing or guaranteeing to do or give something, or not to do or give something, in the future indication of forthcoming excellence or goodness: a writer showing considerable promise the thing of which an assurance is given."

This world is full of people with empty promises. People, friends, love ones and even politicians will promise you of something special... "I'll do this to you if..." "I'll build you the road if..." "Just vote for me and let me serve you and let me be your mayor or governor and... yes, and I will do this... for you." Remember the "Ifs" of the presidents, governors and even common people that never happens. Those are empty promises. Promises were made to be broken by broken people. But this is not true with God. In (Mark 11:22- 25) and notice what He said in these verses:

- "He shall have whatsoever he saith..." in (verse 23)
- "He shall have whatsoever he desires..." in (verse 24) "... Therefore I say unto you, what things soever ye desire..."
- Those things shall come to pass... (verse 23) "...and shall not doubt in his heart, but shall believe that those things which he saith shall come to pass; he shall have whatsoever he saith."

God has the same promises for us and it's from generation to generations. It will never be broken. What God said will surely come to pass. For those who come to Him in prayer with faith in their hearts, remember this… as a believer of the Lord Jesus Christ; we're just one bended knee away from God's miracle and grace. I have failed my wife and my children on some of the promises I made for them as a husband and a dad. But our Dad in heaven will never fail. There was an old song which says, "Jesus Never Fail…" The Lord has promised us of eternal life and of heaven. He promised forgiveness to those who come to Him in repentance. He promised to cleanse us with His precious blood. He promise to provide all our needs according to His riches in glory… and we can go on and on with all the promises of God in the Scriptures. God has promised us His Holy Spirit and He said that He will comfort us and endued us with power. The same Holy Spirit of God that convicted us of our sins; He also comforts us in our journey as Christians. "But the Comforter, which is the Holy Ghost, whom the Father will send in my name, he shall teach you all things, and bring all things to your remembrance, whatsoever I have said unto you." (John 14:26)

We can also take the great words of Apostle Paul in the book of (Romans 4:20 -21) "20- He staggered not at the promise of God through unbelief; but was strong in faith, giving glory to God; 21- And being fully persuaded that, what he had promised, he was able also to perform."

25

FRIDAY

THE PRAYER OF THE DISCIPLES

(Luke 21: 36) "36- Watch ye therefore, and pray always, that ye may be accounted worthy to escape all these things that shall come to pass, and to stand before the Son of man."

Here are some of the unselfish prayers of the disciples in which I believe could be so profitable to Christians, churches and even homes. Twelve things to pray for:

1- That the Lord will give us faith or increase our faith. "And the apostles said unto the Lord, Increase our faith." (Luke 17:5)

2- That we will be strong in the faith. "6- Be strong and of a good courage: for unto this people shalt thou divide for an inheritance the land, which I sware unto their fathers to give them. 7- Only be thou strong and very courageous, that thou mayest observe to do according to all the law, which Moses my servant commanded thee: turn not from it to the right hand or to the left, that thou mayest prosper whithersoever thou goest." (Joshua 1: 6-7)

3- That the Lord will give us grace to pray and receive. "7- Ask, and it shall be given you; seek, and ye shall find; knock, and it shall be opened unto you: 8- For every one that asketh receiveth; and he that seeketh findeth; and to him that knocketh it shall be opened." (Matthew 7: 7- 8)

4- That the Lord will give us the grace to desire the right thing. "Delight thyself also in the LORD; and he shall give thee the desires of thine heart." (Psalms 37:4)

5- That the Lord will give us the grace to forgive. "25- And when ye stand praying, forgive, if ye have ought against any: that your Father also which is in heaven may forgive you your trespasses. 26- But if ye do not forgive, neither will your Father which is in heaven forgive your trespasses." (Mark 11: 25- 26)

6- That people will get saved. "Brethren, my heart's desire and prayer to God for Israel is, that they might be saved." (Romans 10:1)

7- That we pray a Spirit- filled prayer and with the Spirit. "What is it then? I will pray with the spirit, and I will pray with the understanding also: I will sing with the spirit, and I will sing with the understanding also." (I Corinthians 14: 15)

8- That the thoughts of thine heart may be forgiven... "Repent therefore of this thy wickedness, and pray God, if perhaps the thought of thine heart may be forgiven thee." (Acts 8: 22)

9- That we do no evil; not that we should appear approved... "Now I pray to God that ye do no evil; not that we should appear approved, but that ye should do that which is honest, though we be as reprobates." (II Corinthians 13: 7)

10- That God will count you worthy. "Wherefore also we pray always for you, that our God would count you worthy of this calling, and fulfill all the good pleasure of his goodness, and the work of faith with power:" (II Thessalonians 1: 11)

11- That the Word of the Lord may have free course, and be glorified... "Finally, brethren, pray for us, that the word of the Lord may have free course, and be glorified, even as it is with you:" (II Thessalonians 3:1)

12- That we pray one for another. "Confess your faults one to another, and pray one for another, that ye may be healed. The effectual fervent prayer of a righteous man availeth much." (James 5: 16)

SATURDAY
THE PARABLE OF THE DRIED FIG TREE

(Luke 13:6- 9) "6- He spake also this parable; A certain man had a fig tree planted in his vineyard; and he came and sought fruit thereon, and found none. 7- Then said he unto the dresser of his vineyard, Behold, these three years I come seeking fruit on this fig tree, and find none: cut it down; why cumbereth it the ground? 8- And he answering said unto him, Lord, let it alone this year also, till I shall dig about it, and dung it: 9- And if it bear fruit, well: and if not, then after that thou shalt cut it down."

In the Book of (Mark 11:12- 26); we can see here that the Lord Jesus Christ was cursing the fruitless fig-tree. He came to this place for breakfast and to rest a while. The Lord was hungry which I believe was the reason why He went there to eat from the fruits of the fig tree according to (verses 12- 13). Finding himself in want of food, he went to a fig-tree which he saw. And because the fig tree may look so beautiful because of the green leaves, he hoped to find fruit for breakfast from that beautiful tree. But he found nothing but leaves. Jesus hoped to find some fruit, because the gathering of figs was near. But He did not see any fruit and it was one of the very disappointing moments for the Lord to see. It was a good example or illustration of Christ who was willing to come and check of us and spend time with us. He was willing to be there for us as figs; but to His disappointment, He found us fruitless. Christ made an example of it to the men of that generation and the generations to come "…for the time of figs was not yet." According to Matthew Henry; "This was intended to be a type and figure of the doom passed upon the Jewish church, to which he came, seeking fruit, but found none." Compare these verses to the Lord's experienced on the fig tree. "6- He spake also this parable; A certain man had a fig tree planted in his vineyard; and he came and sought fruit thereon, and found none. 7- Then said he unto the dresser of his vineyard, Behold, these three years I come seeking fruit on this fig tree, and find none: cut it down; why cumbereth it the ground? 8- And he answering said unto him, Lord, let it alone this year also, till I shall dig about it, and dung it: 9- And if it bear fruit, well: and if not, then after that thou shalt cut it down." (Luke 13:6- 9) The host in our home Bible study prepared some fruits for us and one of them was figs' fruit. It was funny because the group unconsciously keeps on saying; "The fig tree is so sweet..." and I kept on correcting and telling them that it's not a fig tree, it's a fruit.

Don't let your life, your service, your relationship with God and your church and ministry be dried down by anything or anyone. We cannot afford to have another dry life, dry ministry and a dead church. We must keep the ball rolling for Jesus; be relevant and be on fire for Him. To have another dry life, dry ministry and a dry church is a spiritual disaster.

Paul wrote; "8- (According as it is written, God hath given them the spirit of slumber, eyes that they should not see, and ears that they should not hear;) unto this day. 25- For I would not, brethren, that ye should be ignorant of this mystery, lest ye should be wise in your own conceits; that blindness in part is happened to Israel, until the fullness of the Gentiles be come in." (Romans 11:8, 25)

SUNDAY

WHY TOO MANY RELIGIONS?

(I Peter 2:9- 10) "9- And being fully persuaded that, what he had promised, he was able also to perform. 10- Which in time past were not a people, but are now the people of God: which had not obtained mercy, but now have obtained mercy."

Why too many religions in the world? Do you need a religion to go to heaven or the religion just needs you? Let us cross examine the true meaning of religion. If religion could give us real peace, joy, satisfaction, happiness and salvation; why is it then that the world is still longing for peace, joy, satisfaction, happiness and salvation? If religion is the answer to the spiritual need of men; why is it then that there are millions and millions of people who have religion and still living an empty life and with spiritual emptiness?

What is the Meaning of Religion or True Religion?

What is the root word of religion? What is the difference between religion and the teaching of the Holy Bible? How would you relate religion to belief and the church?

The word *religion* comes from the 2 Latin words which are *"RE"* - *"AGAIN"* and *"LEGEO"* - *"TO TIE"* from which we get the word RELIGION meaning TO TIE AGAIN. Someone said- "It's together again". What are we going to *"tie again"* or to which are we going to be *"tied again"*? To whom are we going to be *"tied again"* or tied back? The Bible said; "For God so loved the world, that he gave his only begotten Son, that whosoever believeth in him should not perish, but have everlasting life." (John 3:16) "Jesus saith unto him, I am the way, the truth, and the life: no man cometh unto the Father, but by me." (John 14:6)

The broken relationship of God and man by sin in the Garden of Eden, when man was tempted by Satan can only be restored or tied back by the death and by the shed blood of the Lamb of God which taketh away the sins of the world. "The next day John seeth Jesus coming unto him, and saith, Behold the Lamb of God, which taketh away the sin of the world." (John 1:29)

According to World English Dictionary; "religion" means:

- *"belief in, worship of, or obedience to a supernatural power or powers considered to be divine or to have control of human destiny,*
- *any formal or institutionalized expression of such belief: the Christian religion,*
- *the attitude and feeling of one who believes in a transcendent controlling power or powers,*
- *chiefly RC Church the way of life determined by the vows of poverty, chastity, and obedience entered upon by monks, friars, and nuns: to enter religion,*
- *something of overwhelming importance to a person: football is his religion,*
- *archaic: a. the practice of sacred ritual observances b. sacred rites and ceremonies, [C12: via Old French from Latin religiō fear of the supernatural, piety, probably from religōre to tie up, from re- + ligōre to bind]" (Internet at Yahoo, World English Dictionary)*

Don't just join in a religion because it's huge, it's lively in their worship and it makes you feel happy or fulfilled. And don't even join that religion because of their music, because they have some dynamic preachers or have a great ministry. Be careful with those who have the charisma and the ability to gather and persuade people to support them financially. James wants for us to have an inside out, soul searching experienced regarding our relationship with God and he wants for us to have the true and pure religion. "26- If any man among you seem to be religious, and bridleth not his tongue, but deceiveth his own heart, this man's religion is vain. 27- Pure religion and undefiled before God and the Father is this, To visit the fatherless and widows in their affliction, and to keep himself unspotted from the world." (James 1: 26- 27)

MONDAY

"BECAUSE THOU HAST LEFT THY FIRST LOVE..."

(Revelation 2:3- 4) "3- And hast borne, and hast patience, and for my name's sake hast laboured, and hast not fainted. 4- Nevertheless I have somewhat against thee, because thou hast left thy first love."

This is the church that Paul started and was developed or was cultivated and watered by John. The Lord Jesus Christ wants to have an intimate relationship with His church. Paul has a good analogy of such intimate relationship of Christ and His church. Apostle Paul wrote to the Ephesians church; "23- For the husband is the head of the wife, even as Christ is the head of the church: and he is the saviour of the body. 24- Therefore as the church is subject unto Christ, so let the wives be to their own husbands in everything. 25- Husbands, love your wives, even as Christ also loved the church, and gave himself for it;" (Ephesians 5: 23- 25) In Revelation chapter two and verse two is an encouragement to us Christians. God is observing and watching us as His children. I remember the classic song which says; "His eyes is on the sparrow..." The Lord's eyes are on His church, so let us be careful and watch our words, our ways and our works. Notice the commendation of Christ to His church, ministers and members. The declaration and the commendation of the King of kings and the Lord of lords to His servants; "I know thy works, and thy labour" God knows your *works* and Christ knows how you have been working hard in (private, for your family) and in (public- in your office, work place, school, church or ministry...). Notice the words *"Labour of love"* or labour for yourself. Is it for self- interest, labour for His sakes, or your labour for righteousness' sakes? It could be labor in *patience*, in tribulation, with people, or in Christian service? Serving God requires patience. We all need patience in tribulation. We need patience while you are waiting for God's time, God's blessings and the answer to your prayers. God knows your works and how you work for Him.

Weakness - "…and how thou canst not bear them which are evil…" In my own opinion; this is a positive kind of weakness. We should all be reminded of the Lord's Words to the churches as stated in verse "7- He that hath an ear, let him hear what the Spirit saith unto the churches; To him that over cometh will I give to eat of the tree of life, which is in the midst of the paradise of God." In his "Morning by Morning" devotional book; Charles Haddon Spurgeon wrote: "If I were dealing with a man's promise, I would carefully consider the ability and the character of the man who had covenanted with me. So with the promise of God; my eye must not be focused as much on the greatness of the mercy- that may stagger me- as on the greatness of the promiser- that will cheer me. My soul, it is God, even your God, God who cannot lie, who speaks to you. This word of His that you are now considering is as true as His own existence. He is an unchangeable God. He has not altered the words that have gone out of His mouth, nor has He called back one single comforting sentence." (Morning by Morning, page 217- July 27) May we stand for God and His Word and maintain our love for Him and His Word.

We must love and be an example of God's love to the unloving world. We also need to labor and work hard out of love. We can claim the same promise as mentioned by Apostle Paul in (Romans 4:21) "And being fully persuaded that, what he had promised, he was able also to perform."

TUESDAY

ALL ABOUT LOVE

(I Corinthians 13:1) "1- Though I speak with the tongues of men and of angels, and have not charity, I am become as sounding brass, or a tinkling cymbal."

I was at the bank and I remember the phrase on a frame which says: "Live well, laugh often, love always". I made a comment and said to the teller about what it says… And in our conversation I said; "It should be the other way around…" "Love always, laugh often and you will live well." She said; "I agree with you…"

I don't know how this world would look like without *love*. If you would just picture in your mind how our homes, our churches and our work place would look like without *love*. The love of God that was shed abroad in the believer's heart is one of the reasons why there is balanced in this sinful, hateful and wicked world. Lydia Maria Child said, "The cure for all the ills and wrongs, the cares, the sorrows and the crimes of humanity, all lie in that one word 'love', it is the divine vitality that everywhere produces and restores life."

Vincent Van Gogh once said, "Love is something eternal".

Apostle Paul the greatest follower of the Lord Jesus Christ in the New Testament times said it well in (I Corinthians 13: 4- 8). Before the Lord created us or before we were born; His love was already been there for us. We may have some lonely days and bad days, but God's love will always be the same. We cannot put God's love in a bucket and keep it in the 4 corners of our home, of our church or organization. The reason why we are here on earth was because of His great love. The reason why Jesus died on the cross and we have salvation in Him was because of His love for us. The reason why He prepared a place for us in heaven is because God wants to be with us, because He loves us so much.

Be it at home, in your work place and even in churches, love is the main thing. It was just because of this one word *"love"; it* changed and turned the world upside down. It was the "love of God". Few years ago, I wrote a song about love. My friend Macky Cordeniel helped me with the music and arrangement. "Love is the Reason" was recorded by my daughter to be used as a theme song for my radio program based in the Philippines and can be heard on the internet. I hope and pray that the message of the song will minister to your heart.

"Love is the reason, love is the key.
Love is what I long for; His love is all I need…
I know that love is everything; I know that love is from God
I know that love bridges my soul to heaven,
God's love nailed Him on the tree…
Sin is the reason, sin brings misery,
His death is the answer, His love reaches me…
We are the reason… that put Him on a tree
But Christ is the answer His greatest love in me"

"6- For when we were yet without strength, in due time Christ died for the ungodly. 7- For scarcely for a righteous man will one die: yet peradventure for a good man some would even dare to die. 8- But God commendeth his love toward us, in that, while we were yet sinners, Christ died for us." (Romans 5: 6- 8)

WEDNESDAY

"THANK YOU"

(Psalm 100: 4- 5) "4- Enter into his gates with thanksgiving, and into his courts with praise: be thankful unto him, and bless his name. 5- For the LORD is good; his mercy is everlasting; and his truth endureth to all generations."

In our morning worship service before I preach; it is my personal practice or some kind of a personal tradition to just seat in front row to pray undisturbed. I meditate and look forward on what God would *DO* in our worship. One Sunday while I have my time with God I came across to a small gospel tract which has been in my Bible for a long time and it says:

> *"THANK YOU!*
> We say it so often
>
> • when a waitress gives us good service
> • when a customer buys our product
> • when someone gives us helping hand
> Sometimes we show as well as say our thanks
> • when we leave a small tip
> • when we send a little gift to a friend or hostess
> • when we give that warm, sincere hand-shake

I'd like to show my appreciation to you by telling you something that is of far greater value. It is simply that the greatest gift in the world can be yours for the asking. That gift is the friendship of my best friend-Jesus Christ. He took away my sin and guilt and gives me joy and peace. I serve him with loving obedience and find in Him my life, my hope, my everything! He invites you, 'Come unto me, all ye that labor and are heavy laden, and I will give you rest.' He saves; He keeps; He satisfies! Introducing Him to you is the best way that I can say **Thank you!**" (Faith, Prayer & Tract League, Grand Rapids, MI 49504)

People will complain of what they don't have and they will also complain of what they have and they want more or better. Contentment, satisfaction, gratefulness… and just be happy are the keys to this kind of attitude. Remember that "Only Jesus Can Satisfy Your Soul". My mother was a grateful and a positive person. She would appreciate everything and I never heard her complain about something or about someone. Every time my wife gave her something; she would really treasure them and take care of them. "Be grateful".

Apostle Paul said; "In everything give thanks: for this is the will of God in Christ Jesus concerning you." (I Thessalonians 5:18)

THURSDAY

SO MUCH TO BE THANKFUL FOR…

(Psalm 105: 1) "O give thanks unto the LORD; call upon his name: make known his deeds among the people."

We have so much to be thankful for… Are you grateful or thankful you're being used by God in some ways? Are you thankful to God your sins are forgiven and you are free? "If the Son therefore shall make you free, ye shall be free indeed." (John 8:36; I John 1: 7- 9) Our God owns everything, what a blessing to know. "A Psalm of David. The earth is the LORD'S, and the fullness thereof; the world, and they that dwell therein." (Psalms 24:1) "Behold, the heaven and the heaven of heavens is the LORD'S thy God, the earth also, with all that therein is." (Deuteronomy 10:14; Psalms 50:10-11; I Chronicles 29:11-12;) "The silver is mine, and the gold is mine, saith the LORD of hosts."(Haggai 2:8) God owns all the money and wealth of the world including those from the top billionaires and millionaires of our time.

Some people may have not known that we will all be judged by the Lord our God someday unless you repent. Check out what Paul said about it in his writings; "For we must all appear before the judgment seat of Christ; that every one may receive the things done in his body, according to that he hath done, whether it be good or bad." (I Corinthians 4:1-2; II Corinthians 5:10) In our darkest moment, hope is always an option. It's a blessing to know that Jesus is at the other end of the tunnel shining as the light of our darkened world. Like Joseph the son of Jacob; God was the only light in the total darkness of the Well every time he looks up to heaven. Jesus was the only light for Paul and Silas when they were in the dark Dungeon. God has not changed in His dealing with us and He has not changed in what He is doing in us and what He will be doing through us. No matter what we're going through and no matter how hard and painful life could be; we must learn to thank God and just be thankful... Someone out there may be going through something that could be *WORST* than what you're going through right now.

"Enter into his gates with thanksgiving, and into his courts with praise: be thankful unto him, and bless his name." (Psalm 100:4)

FRIDAY

AS GOD'S STEWARDS

(I Corinthians 4: 1- 2) "2- Let a man so account of us, as of the ministers of Christ, and stewards of the mysteries of God. 2- Moreover it is required in stewards, that a man be found faithful."

There's a big difference between the blessings and the things you acquired by your own strength or you acquired in the flesh. Take note of what Solomon says about having God's blessing. "The blessing of the LORD, it maketh rich, and he addeth no sorrow with it." (Proverbs 10:22) We can either work for money or work for God. We can also work to be a blessing or work hard and still put more burdens in our life or in our home. It's an issue about how we express our love and devotion for Christ. Jesus said; "No man can serve two masters: for either he will hate the one, and love the other; or else he will hold to the one, and despise the other. Ye cannot serve God and mammon." (Matthew 6:24) Christ talked about this love, treasures and expression of our devotion in the book of Matthew. (Matthew 6:19- 21) With all the abundance of God's blessings and all the abundance of what God is doing in our lives; our tendency as a human being is to be proud, arrogant, self- sufficient and exalt ourselves instead of giving God the glory. We have the tendency to forget that we are just God's stewards of His blessings, His ministry and His church. We are God's stewards or managers of our *time, treasures and talents.* God entrusted to us our *family, fame and God's prepared fortune for us.* God placed before us our *future, friends and His field to plow and cultivate.*

Apostle Peter wrote; "10- As every man hath received the gift, even so minister the same one to another, as good stewards of the manifold grace of God. 11- If any man speak, let him speak as the oracles of God; if any man minister, let him do it as of the ability which God giveth: that God in all things may be glorified through Jesus Christ, to whom be praise and dominion forever and ever. Amen." (I Peter 4: 10- 11) Even in little things and on things that seems to be of no value; God wants for us to be faithful unto it. (Luke 19: 16- 17)

Do you remember this phrase? "Little is much when God is in it". It's not about how much talents and treasures you have. It's not about how rich or poor you are. It's not even how good, knowledgeable and how many doctorate you have. It's about your heart for God and how you have given everything for the Lord and for His sakes and glory.

Check out on what the richest and wisest man that ever lived said in the book of Proverbs; "16- Better is little with the fear of the LORD than great treasure and trouble therewith. 17- Better is a dinner of herbs where love is, than a stalled ox and hatred therewith." (Proverbs 15:16-17)

SATURDAY
YOUR HOLY AND ACCEPTABLE SERVICE
(ROMANS 12:1- 2) "1- I beseech you therefore, brethren, by the mercies of God, that ye present your bodies a living sacrifice, holy, acceptable unto God, which is your reasonable service. 2- And be not conformed to this world: but be ye transformed by the renewing of your mind, that ye may prove what is that good, and acceptable, and perfect, will of God."

In (Genesis 22:1-18) we have here Abraham took his own son to be a sacrificed up on a mountain as God commanded him to do so. He built an altar upon which to burn him (Isaac). Abraham placed his son to the altar as an act of obedience and faith. Then Abraham heard God's voice and God told him that this was just a test of his faith. However, God still required of him some burnt offering in which God Himself provided a ram for the said offering. We can definitely learn from Abraham's holy and acceptable service and sacrificed for God. He pleased God by his obedience, faith, love and service for God. I know of some Christians who would pray like this; "Lord, here's my life take it because I'm willing to die for you." Or "Whatever God wants for me to do, I'm willing to follow and risks my life even to the danger zones of this life… because I'm willing to die for Christ's sake." But Christ first of all wants for us to love Him and live for Him and not to die for His sake. A soldier may go to war but he's not going to war to die for his country; but to protect, to obey and be truthful and faithful to his duty! As Christ's soldiers, we are here to do more than that. We are to live in His name and be faithful for His sake. The Bible said; "I am crucified with Christ: nevertheless I live; yet not I, but Christ liveth in me: and the life which I now live in the flesh I live by the faith of the Son of God, who loved me, and gave himself for me." (Galatians 2:20) We are crucified with Christ as His disciples. This is a good picture of the believer's mysterious life and standing before God and man. A believer is crucified; yet he live, and he live; yet not him but Christ. So you live for Christ and not die for Him. You are crucified with Christ when you crucify the old man with Him and as you live by the faith of the Son of God. Serving God does not mean you ought to be willing to die for Him; but you ought to be willing to live for Him. God will honor our holy life, our righteousness and our sacrifices for His name's sake. It means that God will accept our offering, our faithful service and labor of love. God wants for us to live a fruitful and useful life. He wants for us to start right, live accordingly and end in a right way or be in the right path. Success for me in the ministry is starting right, keep on doing what is right and end up right. We have pastors and ministries that started right, working and doing what is right during the process of time and after a while... unfortunately end up in the wrong way or wrong direction. A pattern like this happens every day in many parts of the world and the sad part is; millions have not learned their lessons from others who fell into sin or temptation. Jesus wants for us to live our Christian life and be more pleasing in His sight.

Paul's advice to a young preacher Timothy; "But watch thou in all things, endure afflictions, do the work of an evangelist, make full proof of thy ministry." (II Timothy 4: 5)

SUNDAY
YET, IT PLEASED THE LORD...

(Isaiah 53:10) "Yet it pleased the LORD to bruise him; he hath put him to grief: when thou shalt make his soul an offering for sin, he shall see his seed, he shall prolong his days, and the pleasure of the LORD shall prosper in his hand."

We can be *"made accepted"* because we pleased the Lord. (Luke 3:22; Ephesians 2:14-22; II Corinthians 5:14-21). We can please God in our words, in our works and in our ways. "And the Holy Ghost descended in a bodily shape like a dove upon him, and a voice came from heaven, which said, Thou art my beloved Son; in thee I am well pleased." (Luke 3:22) This is one of the things that we cannot fully understand until we get there on the other side of the grave. We will have all the answers in heaven. For God the Father; it pleased Him to bruise Christ. This is really hard to understand or comprehend. The pain, the suffering and the death of the Lord Jesus Christ was acceptable to Him (Hebrews 12:1- 3). He honor, glorify and please God the Father. In (John 8:29) "Then said Jesus unto them, When ye have lifted up the Son of man, then shall ye know that I am he, and that I do nothing of myself; but as my Father hath taught me, I speak these things" May we all can say; "I was made accepted in the beloved and I am well pleasing before my God, Father, Lord and King". The Bible said; "16- And Jesus, when he was baptized, went up straightway out of the water: and, lo, the heavens were opened unto him, and he saw the Spirit of God descending like a dove, and lighting upon him: 17- And lo a voice from heaven, saying, This is my beloved Son, in whom I am well pleased." (Matthew 3:16- 17)

An old Chinese proverb: "...to know ones sorrow you have to walk in their shoes." When Jesus gave Himself to die for our sins; it was not an easy death and it was not even a quick one. He went through a lot of pain. The Bible said that He was bruised and God the Father let grief be on Him. He was a man of sorrow. "Yet it pleased the Lord..." And if we will go through the same trials and tribulations or suffering, we can always say; "yet it pleased the Lord to let me suffer for His sake".

Let's make a little comparison with (Isaiah 53:3- 5; 8, 10 and Hebrews 9:24- 26) "3- He is despised and rejected of men; a man of sorrows, and acquainted with grief: and we hid as it were our faces from him; he was despised, and we esteemed him not. 4- Surely he hath borne our griefs, and carried our sorrows: yet we did esteem him stricken, smitten of God, and afflicted. 5- But he was wounded for our transgressions; he was bruised for our iniquities: the chastisement of our peace was upon him; and with his stripes we are healed. 8- He was taken from prison and from judgment: and who shall declare his generation? for he was cut off out of the land of the living: for the transgression of my people was he stricken. 10- Yet it pleased the LORD to bruise him; he hath put him to grief: when thou shalt make his soul an offering for sin, he shall see his seed, he shall prolong his days, and the pleasure of the LORD shall prosper in his hand.

24- "For Christ is not entered into the holy places made with hands, which are the figures of the true; but into heaven itself, now to appear in the presence of God for us: 25- Nor yet that he should offer himself often, as the high priest entereth into the holy place every year with blood of others; 26- For then must he often have suffered since the foundation of the world: but now once in the end of the world hath he appeared to put away sin by the sacrifice of himself."

MONDAY
REMAIN FAITHFUL TO GOD

(Ephesians 5:1- 2) "1- Be ye therefore followers of God, as dear children; 2- And walk in love, as Christ also hath loved us, and hath given himself for us an offering and a sacrifice to God for a sweet smelling savour."

I remember when I was seated across an ordination council during my ordination in the pastorate or as a minister of the gospel. One of the expected questions (expected questions because this was been asked in every ordination that I've witnessed): "What is your guarantee that you will not leave the ministry? "Do you know that once you are an ordained pastor, it means you're married to the pastorate or ministry? And we were told that we cannot just leave the ministry no matter what will happen in the future because we're married to the pastorate or the ministry. As Christians and children of God, we are all married to Christ. Remember Paul's exhortation in (Ephesians 5: 21- 31) when he talks about Christ's relationship with the church. In (Revelation 22: 17) "And the Spirit and the bride say, Come. And let him that heareth say, Come. And let him that is athirst come. And whosoever will, let him take the water of life freely." It means that we are to remain faithful in the service of the King. It means we must love Him, serve Him and be faithful to Him in every situations and conditions in life. (Romans 12: 1-2) We made a vow when we married our spouse and it should be our *VOWS* to God as we follow Him in His service. No matter what may happen in this world, you will stand up for Jesus! May God will be pleased and honored to each of us Christians before we all get to heaven. "4- Thou hast a few names even in Sardis which have not defiled their garments; and they shall walk with me in white: for they are worthy. 5- He that overcometh, the same shall be clothed in white raiment; and I will not blot out his name out of the book of life, but I will confess his name before my Father, and before his angels." (Revelation 3: 4- 5)

I truly believe that one of the reasons why God don't give us the vision and the dreams as well as His blessings and miracles is because we're not faithful to Him. The Scriptures said; "6- And he said, Hear now my words: If there be a prophet among you, I the LORD will make myself known unto him in a vision, and will speak unto him in a dream. 7- My servant Moses is not so, who is faithful in all mine house. 8- With him will I speak mouth to mouth, even apparently, and not in dark speeches; and the similitude of the LORD shall he behold: wherefore then were ye not afraid to speak against my servant Moses?" (Numbers 12:6- 8) Some Christians make God their second class Master and God. Moses was a faithful servant of God, no wonder God called him; "My servant Moses…" And notice the commendation of God to Moses; "My servant Moses is not so, who is faithful in all mine house." Have you been faithful to God and in His house?

May we live our lives like how Antipas did live his life as mentioned by the Lord Jesus Christ in the book of (Revelation 2:10; 13) "10- Fear none of those things which thou shalt suffer: behold, the devil shall cast some of you into prison, that ye may be tried; and ye shall have tribulation ten days: be thou faithful unto death, and I will give thee a crown of life. 13- I know thy works and where thou dwellest, even where Satan's seat is: and thou holdest fast my name, and hast not denied my faith, even in those days wherein Antipas was my faithful martyr, who was slain among you, where Satan dwelleth."

TUESDAY
JUST A FEW QUESTIONS FOR YOU ABOUT HEAVEN

(John 14:1- 3) "1- Let not your heart be troubled: ye believe in God, believe also in me. 2- In my Father's house are many mansions: if it were not so, I would have told you. I go to prepare a place for you. 3- And if I go and prepare a place for you, I will come again, and receive you unto myself; that where I am, there ye may be also."

Do you believe in God? Do you believe that the God that you believe in is the Creator of the whole world and the whole universe? Do you believe that God has all the power in the world? He is the ultimate power, the only God and there's no one else? Do you believe that God prepared a place for *you*? And that place called heaven was created for *you*... so *you* can be with Him in heaven. And if the God that you believe in created you and He created heaven; then He must be willing and able to take you to His heaven. But why do you still have to strive with your *own strength, religion and good works?* Why do you still put your trust on man's creations, images and idols when you can put your trust in God? This is not about my Biblical beliefs but your practical answers to a personal question. Here are some of the helpful Bible verses to help you understand more about heaven: "And God shall wipe away all tears from their eyes; and there shall be no more death, neither sorrow, nor crying, neither shall there be any more pain: for the former things are passed away." (Revelation 21: 4) "Therefore are they before the throne of God, and serve him day and night in his temple: and he that sitteth on the throne shall dwell among them. 16- They shall hunger no more, neither thirst anymore; neither shall the sun light on them, nor any heat. 17- For the Lamb which is in the midst of the throne shall feed them, and shall lead them unto living fountains of waters: and God shall wipe away all tears from their eyes." (Revelation 7: 15- 17) What a beautiful picture of heaven. "God shall wipe away all tears from their eyes..." What a promise, He shall wipe away all tears from our eyes:

- The tears of great joy. It is the joy of being in the *house of God.*

- The tears of great peace and cares in the *hands of God.*
- The tears of love from the *heart of God* (Ephesians 2:6- 7). *"The Lord made us sit together..."* "5- Even when we were dead in sins, hath made us alive together with Christ (by grace ye are saved). 6 "And hath raised us up together in heavenly places in Christ Jesus;" We claim by faith what Christ has done and what the Word of God says in the Scriptures. We are not there yet in heaven, but by faith and in our spiritual standing with God, we are already there. You have a reserved mansion in heaven. I was talking to someone and I said; "We are here but we were there, because we have a reserved seat in heaven" Have you asked Christ to make a reservation for you in heaven? We are strangers and in a journey in this world. We live here for a while, but we don't belong into this world. We belong in the other world- God's abode in heaven. Jesus said; "2- In my Father's house are many mansions: if it were not so, I would have told you. I go to prepare a place for you. 3- And if I go and prepare a place for you, I will come again, and receive you unto myself; that where I am, there ye may be also." (John 14:2-3) Notice what this song says: "This world is not my home, I'm just a passing through, my treasure are laid up, somewhere beyond the blue, The angels beckoned me from heavens open door, and I can't feel at home in this world anymore." Our Citizenship is in heaven. People migrate and they acquire citizenship in the country they called *home.* Paul's encouraging words: "20- For our citizenship is in heaven, from which also we look for the Savior, the Lord Jesus Christ, 21- Who shall change our lowly body, that it may be fashioned like his glorious body, according to the working by which he is able even to subdue all things unto himself." (Philippians 3:20-21)

WEDNESDAY

FOOLS FOR CHRIST'S SAKE

(I CORINTHIANS 3:18- 20) "18- Let no man deceive himself. If any man among you seemeth to be wise in this world, let him become a fool, that he may be wise. 19- For the wisdom of this world is foolishness with God. For it is written, He taketh the wise in their own craftiness. 20- And again, The Lord knoweth the thoughts of the wise, that they are vain."

Webster's Dictionary- "*fool*" *means* "*one destitute of reason*; a simpleton; *a silly person; a buffoon; to play the look; to triple; to make a fool of; to deceive*". It's good to smile, to laugh and have fun, but it must not be sinful and foolishness. Sometimes foolishness can lead to sin and pain to others. We can be fools for nothing or be fools for the Lord Jesus Christ. Or we can be fools for Satan or be a fool for God. Be a fool for the Word of God or be a fool for the sin of this world and its pleasures. We can be a fool in the sight of God or be a fool in the sight of man. (I Corinthians 1: 18; 20- 21; 24- 25) King David has his own foolishness. (Psalm 38:5; 69: 5) Someone said; "My wounds stink and are corrupt because of my foolishness." People get killed or get in trouble with the law because of their own foolishness. One day we were watching the America's Funniest TV show and it shows how people were doing some crazy things just for the fun of it. Some of them got hurt because of their own crazy ideas and deeds. One of my church members made a comment while enjoying the crazy ideas of others. He said; "It was crazy and non- sense" "The foolishness of man perverteth his way: and his heart fretteth against the LORD." (Proverbs 19:3) If you please the world people will say something negative or will criticize you anyways, as well as when you please your Lord and Master. "Let no man deceive himself. If any man among you seemeth to be wise in this world, let him become a fool, that he may be wise. 19- For the wisdom of this world is foolishness with God. For it is written, He taketh the wise in their own craftiness. 20- And again, The Lord knoweth the thoughts of the wise, that they are vain." (I Corinthians 3:18- 20)

Some people do things that are out of this world. Some will do crazy things that are beyond our imaginations; either for the sake of money, fame or friends. But Christians has all the reasons to be a fool for Christ's sake.

God's children have their own foolishness as what King David said in (Psalm 69:5) "O God, thou knowest my foolishness; and my sins are not hid from thee." This is not the kind of foolishness that Apostle Paul was talking about. This is the foolishness according to the standard and lifestyle of the world. I remember my church member in the Philippines who just finished college with honor. He felt the Lord was calling him to a full time ministry. So he came to his parents and asked them if they would allow him to enroll in a Bible college to be a pastor someday. And his parents who were unbelievers back then said; "Are you crazy? Are you out of your mind? We sacrificed and sent you to college so you could have a better life and help your siblings someday! Now you want to be a pastor... There's no money in the pastorate." The Bible says; "25- Because the foolishness of God is wiser than men; and the weakness of God is stronger than men. 26- For ye see your calling, brethren, how that not many wise men after the flesh, not many mighty, not many noble, are called: 27- But God hath chosen the foolish things of the world to confound the wise; and God hath chosen the weak things of the world to confound the things which are mighty;" (I Corinthians 1:25- 27)

THURSDAY

WE ARE FOOL FOR CHRIST'S SAKE, BECAUSE WE
BELIEVE ON THE GOSPEL FOR OUR SALVATION.
(Proverbs 1:5-7) "5- A wise man will hear, and will increase learning;
and a man of understanding shall attain unto wise counsels:6- To
understand a proverb, and the interpretation; the words of the wise,
and their dark sayings.7- The fear of the LORD is the beginning of
knowledge: but fools despise wisdom and instruction."

King Solomon wrote; "He that trusteth in his own heart is a fool:
but whoso walketh wisely, he shall be delivered." (Proverbs 28:26)
What does it mean to walk wisely? It means we have to live and
make decisions according to the wisdom of God. We don't just
make a decision according to the flesh, but in the Spirit. Jesus said
in (Matthew 10:16) "Behold, I send you forth as sheep in the midst
of wolves: be ye therefore wise as serpents, and harmless as doves."
The Bible says: "For I delivered unto you first of all that which I
also received, how that Christ died for our sins according to the
scriptures; 4- And that he was buried, and that he rose again the
third day according to the scriptures:" (I Corinthians 15:1-5; 1:21)

What is the definition or the meaning of the word *gospel*? Paul
defined gospel as the *death, burial and resurrection of the Lord Jesus
Christ according to the Scriptures.* Believing on what Christ did on the
cross 2,000 years ago for eternal life is foolishness to the unbelieving
world. (Ephesians 2:8-9) Believing in Christ for eternal life sounds
impossible to many. But that's what the Bible says… It was because
of the finished work of Christ. We don't have to make it hard for
ourselves. We don't have to work hard and focus on what we can
do or must do…, because the finished work of Christ on the cross
of Calvary is the only resolution to our sin problem and for our
salvation. People sometimes could not fully understand the power of
the gospel. "21- Because that, when they knew God, they glorified
him not as God, neither were thankful; but became vain in their

imaginations, and their foolish heart was darkened. 22- Professing themselves to be wise, they became fools," (Romans 1: 21-22)

The Apostle Paul reminds us about the gospel as foolishness to the world. It's foolishness indeed for the atheists, the unbelievers or the infidel. To believe in some events at the cross of Calvary more than 2,000 years ago is quite hard to comprehend. It's even more complicated for them to believe in someone that they have not seen or heard and know. But we know that Jesus was born of a virgin, He lived for 33 years here on earth and He died, He was buried and rose from the dead after 3 days.

It would be great if Christians will read and meditate on Paul's writings… "17- For Christ sent me not to baptize, but to preach the gospel: not with wisdom of words, lest the cross of Christ should be made of none effect. 18- For the preaching of the cross is to them that perish foolishness; but unto us which are saved it is the power of God. 19- For it is written, I will destroy the wisdom of the wise, and will bring to nothing the understanding of the prudent. 20- Where is the wise? Where is the scribe? Where is the disputer of this world? Hath not God made foolish the wisdom of this world? 21- For after that in the wisdom of God, the world by wisdom knew not God; it pleased God by the foolishness of preaching to save them that believe." (I Corinthians 1:17- 21)

FRIDAY

LOVE, LOVE, LOVE

(I JOHN 3:14- 18) "14- We know that we have passed from death unto life, because we love the brethren. He that loveth not his brother abideth in death. 15- Whosoever hateth his brother is a murderer: and ye know that no murderer hath eternal life abiding in him. 16- Hereby perceive we the love of God, because he laid down his life for us: and we ought to lay down our lives for the brethren. 17- But whoso hath this world's good, and seeth his brother have need, and shutteth up his bowels of compassion from him, how dwelleth the love of God in him? 18- My little children, let us not love in word, neither in tongue; but indeed and in truth."

In this world we have the needy, the greedy, and those who pity. But we need people, politicians, Christians, and philanthropists who would really put wings on their love for mankind. You will not just say "I love you, sweetheart or honey"; but you have to show it by your deeds- good deeds. People sometimes used those words "I love you" and don't even mean it. Sometimes it becomes a byword. I remember an old song… "Love is a many splendored things…" But to others, it's "Love is a many splitters… things." It's not just splitters but splinters to some husbands or wives. Sounds funny but it's true to many people. Divorce, separations and broken marriages are common words to many homes and families. They thought they made a big mistake of marrying their spouse because of their differences or because they don't get what they want. If you love someone; you must be willing to sacrifice and make sacrifices for that someone whom you loved. God made a sacrifice through His Son the Lord Jesus Christ, and He sacrificed Himself because of His love for us. "So, let us not love in words, neither in tongue; but in deeds and truth". You will set aside your problem with money, personal differences, pride, insecurity, and fear in the name of *love*. The Beatles has a song which says, "Love, love, love…"

There are (2) John 3: 16 in the Bible which talks about *love*. The first one is in (John 3: 16) "For God so loved the world, that he gave his only begotten Son, that whosoever believeth in him should not perish, but have everlasting life." And the other one is in (I John 3: 16) "Hereby perceive we the love of God, because he laid down his life for us: and we ought to lay down our lives for the brethren." Success means *L-O-V-E*:

- Living for God.
- Obey His will.
- Value God's Word and your family.
- Encourage others to do the same.

We ought to love God, love the brethren and love our neighbors. It means that it would be both the believers and the unbelievers. In Miami International Airport there's a sign which says, "All you need is love." That's what your wife, your children and your fellowmen as well as your church needs– *LOVE*. That's one of the hardest parts to exercise in the name of Christianity. You need the grace of God to do such because there are people out there who will be hard on you, rude and don't really care.

Apostle Paul in his Epistle wrote; "7- For God hath not given us the spirit of fear; but of power, and of love, and of a sound mind." (II Timothy 1:7)

SATURDAY
"BE A WITNESS"
(Matthew 28:19- 20) "19- Go ye therefore, and teach all nations, baptizing them in the name of the Father, and of the Son, and of the Holy Ghost: 20- Teaching them to observe all things whatsoever I have commanded you: and, lo, I am with you alway, even unto the end of the world. Amen."

Reverend Juan Holguin was our speaker in our church. Rev. Holguin was sharing to us in our worship service about God's principles. Reverend Holguin was talking about the time when God called us to His vineyard. And he was referring to the Scripture in the book of (Matthew 28:19- 20). Pastor Holguin said "…even before we get to the place where God called us to minister, He was already there waiting for us." What a promised that God has for us. God knows where we can serve Him best and He knows what He has in stored for us in His vineyard and all we have to do is to obey Him and trust Him for the results. I remember when I was waiting, seeking and was trying to get the feel where God wants for me to serve. And I was at the convention of our State here in Michigan when I had the confirmation from the Lord to start or *re-start* the work in Trenton, Michigan. It was a preaching from (Psalms 1:1-6). Verse 3 was used by the Lord when He touched me and leads me to His work, His will and His timing. I asked the Lord at that time that He would plant me there at the city of Trenton. I have the assurance from the Lord that if it be His will for me to start the church again; it means that He will give me the grace, the strength, and good foundation. And the Bible says, "…his leaf also shall not wither…" I asked God that it would not be another church or another dry church. I desire to start a church that would make an impact, a church that will influence and touch people's lives. "…and whatsoever he doeth shall prosper." One of our desires would be to prosper in all that God wants for us to do for His name and His glory. "And God will be with you at the end of the age…" Wow! Isn't that great? How about you? Is God working in your life? Let God work in you and through you as you serve Him in any ways you can. Someone said; "When you come to the Lord, He will never send you away empty unless you come so stuffed full of yourself that there isn't room for any of His blessing."- Youth for Christ Magazine.

Please meditate on the following verses and listen to God's voice from these portions of the Scriptures. (Psalm 1:3) "And he shall be like a tree planted by the rivers of water, that bringeth forth his fruit in his season; his leaf also shall not wither; and whatsoever he doeth shall prosper." When something spectacular is happening some people would want to be the first one to witness. And sometimes we have the tendency to grab the honor of taking the stand to be a witness to a special event, for special person or to a historic event. But as the children of God; have we ever think and passionately desire and intentionally try to witness to the lost? We can be a witness by our words, in our works, through God's Word, in our ways and by God's miracle in us and through us. It's so sad that millions are dying every day without Christ and are lost. Let us do our best in evangelizing our world for Christ and be a part in building the Lord's Kingdom.

In the Book of (Acts 1:8 and Mark 16:15) "8- But ye shall receive power, after that the Holy Ghost is come upon you: and ye shall be witnesses unto me both in Jerusalem, and in all Judaea, and in Samaria, and unto the uttermost part of the earth."; "15- And he said unto them, Go ye into all the world, and preach the gospel to every creature."

MONDAY

ARE YOU WILLING TO FOLLOW CHRIST?

(I Thessalonians 1:6- 8) "6- And ye became followers of us, and of the Lord, having received the word in much affliction, with joy of the Holy Ghost: 7- So that ye were ensamples to all that believe in Macedonia and Achaia. 8- For from you sounded out the word of the Lord not only in Macedonia and Achaia, but also in every place your faith to God-ward is spread abroad; so that we need not to speak anything."

We have a duty as God's children. Our duty is to live a godly life. You may want to remember the SSS of Christianity. It's not the *saved, seat and satisfied*. It is *saved, separated* from sin, lusts of the flesh and worldly pleasures that displeased the Lord and *surrender* your life to God. Your willingness to follow Christ will require you to live godly and practice godliness. You will have to live a life of full surrender of yourself to God. We also need to lay down a good foundation in our *heart*, in our *home* and in the *house* of God. We must first give our own selves unto the Lord. "And this they did, not as we hoped, but first gave their own selves to the Lord, and unto us by the will of God." (2 Corinthians 8:5) We need to practice our duty and faithful obedience to God and His Word. In the book of Genesis chapter two and verse seven it says; "And the LORD God formed man of the dust of the ground, and breathed into his nostrils the breath of life; and man became a living soul." Paul was telling us that our body must be presented to Him holy and blameless. The body is for the Lord and the Lord for the body. Paul said; "Meats for the belly, and the belly for meats: but God shall destroy both it and them. Now the body is not for fornication, but for the Lord; and the Lord for the body. 14- And God hath both raised up the Lord, and will also raise up us by his own power." (I Corinthians 6: 13- 14) We are duty bound and we must be willing to come to the altar of the throne of God and offer our lives and whole being to God and God alone. Paul said; "...ye present your bodies a living sacrifice, holy, acceptable unto God, which is your reasonable service." As much as Christ voluntarily offered us His life and His whole being for the salvation of our souls; it's just right and by God's grace we must offer our bodies to Him. If Apostle Peter followed Jesus by walking on the water; why can't we follow Him by walking in His pathway, by doing His will and by working in His field? If Jesus can make Peter walked in a troubled sea, the same Jesus can make you walk in your troubled sea. Conquer your fear as you follow Christ by looking at the Author and Finisher of our faith. Put God's perspective on the top and in your priority list. God indeed wanted for us to follow Him in everything that He's doing in our lives and in the lives of those around us. To follow the Lord would mean giving your all to God unselfishly and without any reservation. You follow God even if it would cost you your fortune and fame. Follow the Lord whatever it takes and according to His Word and His will. (Luke 9:57- 62)

The Bible says; "19- What? Know ye not that your body is the temple of the Holy Ghost which is in you, which ye have of God, and ye are not your own? 20- For ye are bought with a price: therefore glorify God in your body, and in your spirit, which are God's." (I Corinthians 6:19- 20)

TUESDAY
BE WILLING TO YOUR CALLING

(Luke 9:57- 58; 62) "57- And it came to pass, that, as they went in the way, a certain man said unto him, Lord, I will follow thee whithersoever thou goest. 58- And Jesus said unto him, Foxes have holes, and birds of the air have nests; but the Son of man hath not where to lay his head. 62- And Jesus said unto him, No man, having put his hand to the plow, and looking back, is fit for the kingdom of God."

When you present your bodies you don't present to God a dirty, and defile life. You present to God that which is holy, undefiled and clean bodies. (1 Corinthians 6: 17- 20) We have to worship God through our bodies and yield in His Spirit. We have to love righteousness and holiness inside out. We must offer our life and all in the holy temple of God which is our bodies by giving and dedicating it to God and God alone. We gave and dedicate our whole lives and soul to God by our love, worship and service. "Ye shall not eat of anything that dieth of itself: thou shalt give it unto the stranger that is in thy gates, that he may eat it; or thou mayest sell it unto an alien: for thou art an holy people unto the LORD thy God. Thou shalt not seethe a kid in his mother's milk." (Deuteronomy 14:21) Notice the phrase; *"… for thou art an holy people unto the LORD thy God."* We don't sacrifice our dead body, but our holy life to God. It is a life wherein Christ is living in our soul by faith, which makes the body a living sacrifice as you obey His voice. That is our calling in which God expect of us to be willing to obey and sacrifice. (Galatians 2:20) Paul's life was under the power and authority of God. Paul lived his life not in the flesh, but in the Spirit by which he was conformed in both to the nature and will of God. And even our bodies must not be made as the instruments of sin and uncleanness. We were set apart for God, and we were called to live a holy life. We must be willing to obey and be faithful to our calling. No looking back to sin and worldly pleasures. No looking back to the former world and worldly life. We have to follow Christ and walk straight in His path. We have decided

to follow Jesus therefore: "No turning back, no turning back..."
We must be willing to do God's will by being obedient and faithful
to our calling. God will not ask you someday if you're as successful
as your next door neighbors or you're as great as your co- workers
or fellow ministers. The ministry may not go well with you, but
your job is to obey. Your finances could be on the *red scale* and the
family may not be very supportive to your cause but your job is to
be willing to your calling. Where you may be in right now is out of
control and it's not what you've expected it to be... You still need to
be faithful to your calling and be willing to obey whatever it takes.
Sometimes the series of events and circumstances in our lives and
in the ministry as well as in our calling contradicts or opposite to
what we're expecting to happen; but again we need to be willing to
our calling. Take note of the words of Peter in (I Peter 2:9- 10) "9-
But ye are a chosen generation, a royal priesthood, an holy nation,
a peculiar people; that ye should show forth the praises of him who
hath called you out of darkness into his marvellous light: 10- Which
in time past were not a people, but are now the people of God: which
had not obtained mercy, but now have obtained mercy." God placed
us to where we are right now because He has a purpose. If you really
love the Lord, being willing to obey to God's calling for you and
the issue of faithfulness would not be a problem. And you will take
God seriously! Apostle Paul wrote; "For the gifts and calling of God
are without repentance." (Romans 11:29)

WEDNESDAY
LOVE THE LORD YOUR GOD

(MARK 12:30) "30- And thou shalt love the Lord thy God with all thy heart, and with all thy soul, and with all thy mind, and with all thy strength: this is the first commandment."

The most important thing for us Christians to do is to love God. That's what the Bible says. When Jesus was asked by the people during His time which was the greatest commandment...? The Lord Jesus Christ answered them to "Love the LORD their God..." (Mark 12:30) "And thou shalt love the Lord thy God with all thy heart, and with all thy soul, and with all thy mind, and with all thy strength: this is the first commandment." And this verse was actually from the Old Testament in the book of (Deuteronomy 6:4-6). What would it be like to have a relationship with an opposite sex; be it a husband and wife relationship or a boyfriend-girlfriend relationship and nobody knows about that bonding or relationship; because the couple kept it secret? What would you feel if you don't see your husband or your wife expressed their feelings? It's natural to an average and normal person to express their love to their love ones or love life. We can always look back in the past with our eyes focus on God's faithfulness to us. We can always look back to what He has done in the past and give Him the glory for all the things that God has done for you. It's for Him and all because of Him anyways. Whatever God has done for us, He did it and will continue to do it because of His love for us. The Lord deserves our sacrifices as we give the honor and the glory in His name. If you love the Lord, you would not be ashamed of Him. You desire to express that love in many ways as possible. Some of the best way to express our love is through our *obedience to God*. And that is *obedience to His Word or His commandments*. There will be billions of people out there who are almost at the door of heaven but won't make it there. Some of them will reject the Lord while others were out there in the church out of curiosity. Some were in the church or were involved in religious activities, but they refused to love the Lord. And this could be the same words that Jesus will say to them in (Matthew 12: 34) "And when Jesus saw that he answered discreetly, he said unto him, Thou art not far from the kingdom of God. And no man after that durst ask him any question."

I recently was talking to a friend of mine who is a pastor of the fastest growing church here in Michigan area. I asked him point blank on how he made his church grow and what was his "hocus pocus" if there was one. He said; "Ely, there is no hocus pocus and no formula for this, but to love the Lord, love God's people and love what you're doing for God."

Mister Wynn Davis in his book "The Best of Success" used some of the great quotes about *love* from great people of the centuries: "Life in abundance comes only through great love." Elbert Hubbard

"Love is the immortal flow of energy that nourishes, extends and preserves. Its eternal goal is life." Smiley Blanton

"Love is the emblem of eternity: it confounds all notion of time: effaces all memory of a beginning, all fear of an end." Anna louise De stael

"Take away love and our earth is a tomb." Robert Browning
Do you keep His Word and obedient to Him as your Lord and Master?

"If ye love me, keep my commandments." (John 14:15)

THURSDAY
PRAY, PRAY AND PRAY
(I THESSALONIANS 5:17-18) "17- Pray without ceasing. 18- In everything give thanks: for this is the will of God in Christ Jesus concerning you."

Prayer is our way of communicating with God and it's our way of expressing our love for the Lord. The cops will say these words when they busted someone for the crime they committed; "You have the right to remain silent…" or "Anything you say may be used against you…" But it's not true with the Lord our God. Once you become a Christian, you always have the right to talk to God and talk to people about God. If you committed sins, God wants you to confess your sins to Him and ask God for forgiveness. He will not use any sin that you confessed in the altar of the throne of grace against you as His child.

When you read God's Word, you let God talk to you and when you pray, you are talking to God. When you witness, you talk to them about Jesus and for Jesus. I don't know what you would feel if your spouse would not talk to you without any valid reason. You eat on the same table, shared the same bed and the communication is cut off because there is *no signal*? Is it because your spouse made a bad decision or made a mistake and you used it against your spouse? And as a couple, you're sitting on the same couch, sleeping in the same bed and driving with your spouse next to you… quite, because you just don't want to talk. You would not be happy with your relationship if you keep your ears closed. Just imagine if we're not talking to God about our problems, about our needs, about what He did to us and if we're not thankful to Him. If it hurts us or if we're not pleased because our spouse won't talk to us, I believe God would not be pleased if you will not pray.

Andrew Murray said: "Prayer is not monologue, but dialogue. God's voice in response to mine is its most essential part." Andrew

Murray 1828-1917. This is one of the mistakes and failures of many unbelievers and Christians alike- to pray. Many people and countries in the world pray but in a wrong god. People pray in the name of the saints or in a wrong person. Remember the story of Daniel during the time of Nebuchadnezzar in (Daniel 3), Nebuchadnezzar made a declaration or a law where people were commanded to worship the image that he made. And Daniel and the three young Hebrews refused to worship the god of Nebuchadnezzar. God will spare a nation, a home or an individual if we learn to pray. Remember during the time of Abraham; God talked to Abraham about the destruction of Sodom and Gomorrah because of their pride and immorality. (Genesis 18:20-33) In my speaking engagement, I was asked by a pastor about my physical position when I pray and I said; "I pray face down in my bed" He asked me; "Are we not supposed to be kneeling down when we pray?" Prayer is not about your physical position, it's about your serious and loving communication with a holy God.

The Bible says; "My sheep listen to my voice; I know them, and they follow me." (John 10:27) What God has promised us, He is able to perform and He is faithful in His Words and His promised to His children in the Holy Bible! Our duties and responsibilities are to trust, obey and claim it in Jesus' name. (Romans 4:20- 21) Jesus said; "7- Ask, and it shall be given you; seek, and ye shall find; knock, and it shall be opened unto you: 8- For every one that asketh receiveth; and he that seeketh findeth; and to him that knocketh it shall be opened." (Matthew 7:7- 8)

FRIDAY
WORSHIP GOD IN PRAYER
(ISAIAH 56:7) "7- Even them will I bring to my holy mountain, and make them joyful in my house of prayer: their burnt offerings and their sacrifices shall be accepted upon mine altar; for mine house shall be called an house of prayer for all people."

People sometimes would say that they don't need to pray because God knows their needs anyways. But prayer is not merely asking for something you need from the Lord, it's communicating and building a good and intimate relationship with our Savior. Communication is important to the health of any relationships; especially for husbands and wives, parents and children and even at work. As believers, to have an intimate relationship with God the Father, we need to pray. It's almost impossible to have a close relationship with someone you rarely communicate with. We come to God not to complain to Him or to give Him some info and to tell Him what we want for Him to *do* for us. But we come to the throne of grace to make our relationship with God be sweeter, more intimate, deepen, and stronger. And for a good relationship to be more intimate, it needs to be primarily positive communications. If you want to deepen your relationship with your spouse, then learn to establish an open and positive communication with your spouse. That's what we're supposed to do with our relationship with God. That's the reason why we need to pray and pray constantly. The Apostle Paul wrote, "Pray without ceasing." That is an invitation to fellowship. That is an invitation for communication with God. God desires a meaningful, intimate relationship with us. We can express our love for Him through prayer. Prayer is the only way in which we can communicate our heart to Him and seek to know Him better. Prayer is a central part of worship. In fact, it is the main purpose of coming to the house of God. We come unto the throne of God because we love Him and desire to be in His presence. King David in the Book of Psalm said; "Hear my prayer, O LORD, give ear to my supplications: in thy faithfulness answer me, and in thy righteousness." This may sound like an exaggeration or this may sound impossible to many; but it is seriously true and that's the truth of the Word of God. God answers every prayer of every believer all over the world. "If ye abide in me, and my words abide in you, ye shall ask what ye will, and it shall be done unto you." (John 15:7) This is self- explanatory because the essence of the verse is very elementary in its message. It means that even the grade school students will fully understand. And who can refute these promises from the Scriptures: "O thou that hearest prayer, unto thee shall all flesh come." (Psalm 65:2) Revival starts from the heart of a Christian who humbly prayed to God in repentance and with a broken heart for the Lord and in His Word, it is the longing of the children of God with an inner desire to worship the Lord in Spirit and in truth. Revival is the inner longing of God's people for His presence and glory.

The prophet Isaiah wrote; "Even them will I bring to my holy mountain, and make them joyful in my house of prayer: their burnt offerings and their sacrifices shall be accepted upon mine altar; for mine house shall be called an house of prayer for all people." (Isaiah 56:7) Jesus said; "But thou, when thou prayest, enter into thy closet, and when thou hast shut thy door, pray to thy Father which is in secret; and thy Father which seeth in secret shall reward thee open" (Matthew 6:6)

SATURDAY

GIVING HIM PRAISE AND THE GLORY

(Psalms 103:1- 2) "1- A Psalm of David. Bless the LORD, O my soul: and all that is within me, bless his holy name. 2- Bless the LORD, O my soul, and forget not all his benefits:"

In the Book of (Psalms 92:1) "It is a good thing to give thanks unto the LORD, and to sing praises unto thy name, O most High." Also in the following verses it says; "3- Let them praise thy great and terrible name; for it is holy." 5- "Exalt ye the LORD our God, and worship at his footstool; for he is holy." 9- "Exalt the LORD our God, and worship at his holy hill; for the LORD our God is holy." It means by giving Him thanks not just in the midst of blessing but even in hardships and in pain or sickness. (Psalms 99:3; 5; 9) Apostle Paul has a similar message; "In everything give thanks; for this is the will of God in Christ Jesus concerning you." (I Thessalonians 5:18) I like this:

> "In some of the thing give thanks…
> In something, give thanks…
> In good things, give thanks…
> In my personal thing, give thanks…
> In worthy thing, give thanks…
> In several things, give thanks…
> In most of the thing, give thanks…
> In God's thing, give thanks…
> In your thing, give thanks…
> It's, In everything, give thanks…"

We have so much to be thankful with or so much to be thankful for… There's a hymn which says, "Count your many blessings and name them one by one…" But we have countless blessings that we can't even name them already. Whatever you have at home, in your office, at church give God the praise and the glory for it. Sometimes we do things unconscious of the Lord's presence and not knowing that God have a personal interest on whatever we do and whatever we have in Him and for Him. And it would always be for His name and for His glory. We have here the Lord's Prayer in (John 15:1; 4- 5) It means you give praise to God in everything; "18- In everything give thanks: for this is the will of God in Christ Jesus concerning you." ... (I Thessalonians 5:18) 1- "Praise ye the LORD. Sing unto the LORD a new song, and his praise in the congregation of saints. 2- Let Israel rejoice in him that made him: let the children of Zion be joyful in their King. 3- Let them praise his name in the dance: let them sing praises unto him with the timbrel and harp." (Psalm 149:1- 3) He was in the dark dungeon and in chained with the jailer watching over him. He was waiting for his trial and was expecting a death penalty. Some of his friends deserted him and some of the churches he started did not support him and did not even dare to visit him and comfort him. But notice the words of the great Apostle Paul; "6- Be careful for nothing; but in everything by prayer and supplication with thanksgiving let your requests be made known unto God. 7- And the peace of God, which passeth all understanding, shall keep your hearts and minds through Christ Jesus. 8- Finally, brethren, whatsoever things are true, whatsoever things are honest, whatsoever things are just, whatsoever things are pure, whatsoever things are lovely, whatsoever things are of good report; if there be any virtue, and if there be any praise, think on these things." (Philippians 4:6- 8)

SUNDAY
SEPARATED OR SEPARATISTS?

(I Corinthians 6:15- 17) "15- Know ye not that your bodies are the members of Christ? shall I then take the members of Christ, and make them the members of an harlot? God forbid. 16- What? Know ye not that he which is joined to an harlot is one body? For two, saith he, shall be one flesh. 17- But he that is joined unto the Lord is one spirit."

The moment you present (dedicated, offer) your life to God for Christian service, God has set you up for His glory and separated you from the world. God wants us to live a holy life. He wants for us to live a Christ-like life. Sometimes we need to exercise our practical theology. As Matthew Henry put it this way; "It is the practical application of doctrinal truths that is the life of preaching. When you gave your bodies as a living sacrifice, it means you must be: 1- Active in the Service of the King. 2- You are working for God and you're at your best for Jesus. 3- You walk the talk and talk the walk. The particular exhortations of this chapter are reducible to the three principal heads of Christian duty: our duty to God, to ourselves, and to our brother. The grace of God teaches us, in general, to live godly, soberly, and righteously; and to deny all that which is contrary hereunto. Now this chapter will give us to understand what godliness, sobriety, and righteousness, are though somewhat intermixed." (The Bible Collection Suite)

As a believer of the Lord Jesus Christ, you can make a difference... "And of some have compassion, making a difference:" (Jude 1:22) When I was a pastor of a small church in the Philippines, some of my friends from the other group would not come to my church anniversary and other special church celebrations or functions for only 1 reason; they want to separate themselves from our group and other Christians. And they were my friends, but they don't want to fellowship with us in our worship because we were different from them. And they used this word "separatist". Jesus ate with the publicans and sinners. He talked and dined with sinners, but Jesus did not sin or did He condone their sin. *Resist* the work of the ungodly. Resist the advice and the offer of the evil men. Resist your fleshly desires and the lust of the flesh. This sinful world will offer us temporary pleasures and satisfaction. Be careful of the deceitful works of Satan. Resist Satan's destructive and deceitful offer. God has a better plan for you. You don't need to be a separatist to be acceptable to God. You are a sinner saved by grace. Let us be the servants of God and be a man or woman of the Word. God would love to see you and me following His footsteps for His name and His glory. Be a living sacrifice for our Lord and Savior. You are your best offering and sacrifice for God and His service. It's so unfortunate that Christians, especially the Baptists are divided. We are divided over the issue of Bible translations, form of worships, music in worships and even in a minor detail of the church building and other unnecessary issues. Notice the words of Apostle Paul; "1- Be ye therefore followers of God, as dear children; 2- And walk in love, as Christ also hath loved us, and hath given himself for us an offering and a sacrifice to God for a sweet smelling savour." (Ephesians 5: 1- 2)

MONDAY
THE LORD IS MY SHEPHERD

(John 10:9- 11) "9- I am the door: by me if any man enter in, he shall be saved, and shall go in and out, and find pasture. 10- The thief cometh not, but for to steal, and to kill, and to destroy: I am come that they might have life, and that they might have it more abundantly. 11- I am the good shepherd: the good shepherd giveth his life for the sheep."

On a special occasion or celebrations like Christmas or birthdays; have you ever been asked by a family member, friend or someone special a question like; "What do you want for Christmas or for your birthday?" I was asked several times by my children and my wife and my response was: "The LORD is my Shepherd; I shall not want..." This is true not only for me but to many of us Christians. The more you grow in His grace, the more you put little value of temporal things and put more value on the things of God. In my own opinion and observation, I believe Psalms chapter twenty three and verse one is the Old Testament counterpart of what Paul was talking about in the New Testament, he said; "Not that I speak in respect of want: for I have learned, in whatsoever state I am, therewith to be content." (Philippians 4:11)

The reasons why Christians have satisfaction, joy and peace is because of the Shepherd of shepherds that is in us; who gave us salvation through His shed blood on the cross for our sins. God took away our sins and sinfulness and He changed our heart. He gave us new focus, new perspective and the new Spirit that is in us. The reason why people are living in *want* and *discontentment* is because they don't have the Lord who is our Shepherd.

Paul said; "for I have learned... to be content." in which I believe should be one of the major thing that we need to learn as Christians. Paul learned his lessons considering the pain, hardships, sufferings and imprisonment that he went through, yet Paul said, "... in whatsoever state I am, therewith to be content." There's nothing more important for you and me but the Lord, especially if you're in the brink of downfall or in the valley of the shadow of death.

Let me share to you something that might encourage you when the road of life is rough and life is getting tough for you: "It doesn't matter if it's rainy or sunny, just be happy. And it doesn't matter if it's hilly or you're in the valley, don't be lonely. God is your Shepherd and before you get there in your trials and sufferings or destinations; He was there already waiting for our coming." I would rather live a life destitute of the world's goodness and wealth than to live a life destitute of the presence of God." "Abound" means "to be satisfied and content in the midst of necessities and extremities in life." It is the grace of God which makes you stand and look forward with a positive outlook in life. Jesus is our true contentment. He is our only satisfaction, the source of peace and joy no matter what's going on in our lives.

The Bible says; "5- Let your conversation be without covetousness; and be content with such things as ye have: for he hath said, I will never leave thee, nor forsake thee. 6- So that we may boldly say, The Lord is my helper, and I will not fear what man shall do unto me." (Hebrews 13: 5- 6)

TUESDAY

BE GENEROUS

(Psalms 23: 5- 6) "5- Thou preparest a table before me in the presence of mine enemies: thou anointest my head with oil; my cup runneth over. 6- Surely goodness and mercy shall follow me all the days of my life: and I will dwell in the house of the LORD forever."

Let me share a beautiful story and full of spiritual lessons. It's about the 2 boys who were best friends for a long time. They have 2 different personalities, characters and attitude. Friend number one was a good, nice, not selfish and positive boy. We may say he's almost perfect in his attitude, lifestyle, character, moral value and his outlook in life. He was *generous* and compassionate kind of individual. But boy number two was the opposite. He was a bad, selfish and negative boy. He spent his life for his own and he didn't care about others. He has the "I" "Me" "My" attitude. One day as they were walking in the woods… they met an old, old woman. The woman showed them 2 sets of tables with golden spoons, forks, etc. One of the tables was long and everything on it. And the other one were all regular sizes. And the good news was; the woman was giving them away to the boys. The old woman first asked the boy number 1 to make a choice or pick his table. And to her surprised boy number 1 turned the opportunity to his friend. And to make the long story short, boy number 2 made a choice and he picked the golden long table with all the golden kitchen wares on it. Boy number 2 did not realized that everything they picked would be theirs even after death. You may think… Wow! That was even great and a great deal too, it's free! No, it was not a good deal and it was not great, because the 12 foot long of spoons, forks, knives, glasses and cups and the 30 foot long table will be his in eternity. Boy number 2 will eat from those in eternity. How can he feed himself with those long golden table wares? That was the problem and that's what he got for being selfish, greedy, discontent and for having the wrong value. Did you notice the difference between the 2 and their destiny? May we would have the heart like King David who said: "Thou preparest a table before me in the presence of mine enemies..." (Psalms 23:5) Let the Lord shower you with His blessings and be a channel of those blessings. Let's picture ourselves having the 12 foot long utensils in our hands and with all the good food on our 30 foot long table and the only requirement was for us to eat using the golden table wares (spoons and forks etc.) to feed ourselves. That would be impossible to feed yourself with those long utensils and the only way for us to be fed is to share one another's food, time and utensils by feeding one another. As God's children, we let the Lord prepare the table for us. We let Him prepare the blessing before us. Let God prepare the ministry before you... God will not lead us to greener pastures if we are selfish and if we do not let the good Shepherd lead us. Not only that God's blessing awaits you, but His goodness and mercy will follow you. Notice the testimony of King David, he said; "Thou preparest a table before me in the presence of mine enemies: thou anointest my head with oil; my cup runneth over." (Psalms 23:5) So what do you want to do? Do you want to do it God's way? It means you let Him prepare the table for you. You will let God do the work for you. You will let God work in you and through you by sharing, giving or by being generous and not being selfish. Are you going to do it your way? It means "I" "Me" "My" attitude. The Bible says; "8- For my thoughts are not your thoughts, neither are your ways my ways, saith the LORD. 9- For as the heavens are higher than the earth, so are my ways higher than your ways, and my thoughts than your thoughts." (Isaiah 55:7- 9)

WEDNESDAY
LET GOD PREPARE THE MINISTRY FOR YOU

(Joshua 1:1- 2) "1- Now after the death of Moses the servant of the LORD it came to pass, that the LORD spake unto Joshua the son of Nun, Moses' minister, saying, 2- Moses my servant is dead; now therefore arise, go over this Jordan, thou, and all this people, unto the land which I do give to them, even to the children of Israel. Be strong and of a good courage: for unto this people shalt thou divide for an inheritance the land, which I sware unto their fathers to give them."

When I was new in my Christian life, I never thought of God calling me to be a pastor and to be a church planter. And I never thought of planting a new work or a new church in North America, specifically here in the United States. I was 2 months old in my Christian life when I enrolled in a Bible college. I enrolled not to be a pastor but for 2 reasons: first- I have nowhere to go, I was homeless and I don't know where to go. I don't want to live with my cousin whose 10 x 10 foot house in a very poor area gets flooded during high tide in Malabon city in Metro Manila. On some days, the water was just about an inch below our 2 ½ feet high bed. The second reason which is a little bit spiritual or religious; I love to sing and I thought I could sing for God and travel as a singing evangelist which made me want to learn theology so I could be effective. I did not know exactly what I was getting into. But God has a different plans and He has the best idea. God prepared me from there and He can do the same to you. What if God is preparing a table of ministries for you? Are you prepared? Joshua may never have thought of being Moses' successor. He was just an ordinary man who loves his ministry as the assistant to the servant of God- Moses. He may have thought that it was Caleb or Aaron who would be Moses' successor. (Joshua 1:6- 7) We need to plan for the future, we need to set some goals, we need to have a dream and visions and we need to be faithful in the Lord and be the best that we can be. But we must also be aware that the Lord knows better than we do and He knows what's good for us. We must be prepared for what God has in stored for us in the ministry and for the future. Let Him prepare the ministry for you but you must be prepared to what God has for you in the field and in the future. The Father prepared Jeremiah at the potter's house. He prepared David by being a shepherd and by killing the lions and the bears. He prepared Joseph by being a servant when he was growing up physically. Jesus is the way and He knows the way to success and blessings. You let Him leads the way for you as you step onto the ladder of the Lord's prepared ministry and calling for you. If you would think of the servants of God who followed Him in His way, it was not really easy for them. Joshua, Moses, David, Joseph and Jeremiah went through a process, but they let God prepare the ministry for them by letting God working through them. We don't know what God has for us, but we can be secured and be blessed in spite of uncertainties, obstacles, anxiety and other circumstances that are beyond our control. We don't have to be an excellent preacher, a great singer or musician or be a highly intellectual person to be in the arena of God's ministerial job. All we have to do is to be prepared as God prepares the ministry for you. Everything that God has done, what He is doing and will be working in me, they're all beyond my expectations. He has done so much that was not even in my wildest dreams. He can do the same to you. "11- For I know the thoughts that I think toward you, saith the LORD, thoughts of peace, and not of evil, to give you an expected end. 12- Then shall ye call upon me, and ye shall go and pray unto me, and I will hearken unto you. 13- And ye shall seek me, and find me, when ye shall search for me with all your heart." (Jeremiah 29:11- 13)

THURSDAY
"EVERY WISE WOMAN BUILDETH HER HOUSE..."
(Proverbs 14:1) "Every wise woman buildeth her house: but the foolish plucketh it down with her hands."

It's a beautiful verse designed not just for the wise women but for every husband as well. "Every wise woman buildeth her house..." It means a good and responsible wife. Wives should be a channel of blessings to their husbands and children. The wise wives are those who are building their home in the fear of the Lord. They work hard for the success of their children. She is loving, considerate and takes care of the affairs of the family. Here's I believe is a good personal profile of the "wise women" with the "3 P's" of:

1) *Pious-* The good example is Mary the mother of Jesus in the flesh. "41- And it came to pass, that, when Elisabeth heard the salutation of Mary, the babe leaped in her womb; and Elisabeth was filled with the Holy Ghost: 42- And she spake out with a loud voice, and said, Blessed art thou among women, and blessed is the fruit of thy womb." (Luke 1: 41- 42) Being religious, having religion and a serving wife is different from the holy or pious.

2) *Prosperous-* Prosperity is not about the accumulation of money and things or wealth; it's about keeping your marriage, your home, bringing up your children in the fear of the Lord. The most important thing in life is your relationship with the Lord and with your spouse and children. "The heart of her husband doth safely trust in her, so that he shall have no need of spoil. 28- Her children arise up, and call her blessed; her husband also, and he praiseth her. 30- Favour is deceitful, and beauty is vain: but a woman that feareth the LORD, she shall be praised." (Proverbs 31:11; 28:30) You are living together in happiness, in peace and in the fear of the Lord. You honor His Word in your life. (Joshua 1:8- 9) The wives play a very important role to the family's success and prosperity.

3) *Provider-* In some parts of the world as part of their culture; it is the wives who provides for the needs of the family and it is

the wives who takes care of the homes. In the United States of America, sometimes both parents are working to support the family. In the Philippines, it's expected to be the man who would be the provider. The husband and wives can always be a team player and they should be. When I lost my support and when I lost my job, my wife was the one who provides for the family. It was beyond my control but my wife was more than willing to play my role as a provider for the needs of my children for a while. Reverend Billy Graham was elaborating and answering questions about David's Frost interview about him and Ruth his wife. Mr. Graham quote what Ruth said; "You go preach the gospel, and I'll raise these children for God and you'll be proud of them when they grow up." Providing, protecting and the road to prosperity is a team effort for husbands and wives. "But if any provide not for his own, and especially for those of his own house, he hath denied the faith, and is worse than an infidel." (I Timothy 5: 8) The picture of a good wife and mother is recorded in the book of Proverbs chapter thirty one. Notice what the Bible says; "13- She seeketh wool, and flax, and worketh willingly with her hands. 14- She is like the merchants' ships; she bringeth her food from afar." (Proverbs 31:13- 14)

FRIDAY

GOD'S GOODNESS AND MERCY

(Psalm 97:10) "Ye that love the LORD hate evil: he preserveth the souls of his saints; he delivereth them out of the hand of the wicked."

Celebrating my 30th years in the ministry is all by the grace and mercy of God. It was a few months after I got saved in 1982 when the Lord leads me to witness to people, felt led to minister through the gospel by one on one, in preaching and evangelistic crusades. Based on my personal experienced, I don't remember talking to an individual about eternal life or heaven and they rejected such; not because they don't want to go to a better place or they don't want to go to heaven, but because they don't want to *change*. They don't want to change their religion, their beliefs, their life, their mindset, their bad or evil practices and wickedness. (II Corinthians 5: 17; John 3:3) It's very clear that God wants for us to change and to be born again. Would you be one of the wise men and women of God who hears His Word and obey Him? God wants for us to keep His ways and be wise. You humbly come to God and ask Him to come into your heart. King Solomon was the wisest man on earth and he wrote; "35- For whoso findeth me findeth life, and shall obtain favour of the LORD. 36- But he that sinneth against me wrongeth his own soul: all they that hate me love death." (Proverbs 8:35- 36) God has promised us life, His goodness and mercy, but the decision is in our hands. It's a choice between heaven or hell, life or death. It's for you to choose the cross, the right path, the way to God or the way to darkness and hell. "Jesus saith unto him, I am the way, the truth, and the life: no man cometh unto the Father, but by me." (John 14:6)

Let me share with you this beautiful illustration about mercy compiled by Robert Scott and William C. Stiles:

The Limitation of Mercy
Says the old hymn: While the lamp holds out to burn,
The vilest sinner may return.

An old Saxon king had some serious trouble with his subjects: they murmured against him and at the last rose up in rebellion. The king set out to subdue them, and soon the well-disciplined troops won a decided victory over the tatterdemalion horde opposing them. Having conquered, the king determined to show mercy. He adopted the novel expedient of placing a candle in the window of his castle and proclaiming that all should be pardoned who returned "while the candle burns." (CYCLOPEDIA OF ILLUSTRATIONS For Public Speakers, Funk and Wagnalls Company, New York and London 1911)

It's a beautiful picture of God's love, God's goodness, God's grace and His mercy upon us. The Lord had done greater thing and extended His great mercy on us by the death of His Son. But the love of God, His grace and mercy will someday be over; either by death, by His second coming or by a hardened heart. King Pharaoh did that when he refused to listen to Moses and refused to obey the voice of God. "26- Help me, O LORD my God: O save me according to thy mercy: 8- The LORD is gracious, and full of compassion; slow to anger, and of great mercy. 1- Therefore seeing we have this ministry, as we have received mercy, we faint not;" (Psalm 109:26; 145:8; II Corinthians 4:1)

SATURDAY
THE GREATEST LOVE

(John 3:16) "16- For God so loved the world, that he gave his only begotten Son, that whosoever believeth in him should not perish, but have everlasting life."

There's no greater love but the love of God. It's a kind of love that is beyond our imagination and we cannot comprehend such love. We cannot picture or paint God's love in a canvas. Words cannot express God's love for sinful men like us. In the Bible, Paul was talking about our relationship with the Lord Jesus Christ and eternal life that cannot be broken up by anybody or anything, at anytime and anywhere or by any circumstances in life, (I Corinthians 1:8- 9). Our whole being is in the hands of God the Father and in the Lord Jesus Christ which is sealed by the Holy Spirit of God until the day of redemption, it means until that day when we see Him face to face. What a glory that will be. (I Thessalonians 5:23- 24) You have heard His voice when you responded to His call for you to come to Him and follow Him for your salvation. If you do that, you are therefore with no doubt the son of the living God. What comes along with that is the promised of eternal life in heaven that cannot be taken away from you by sin, Satan and the world system. Jesus said; "27- My sheep hear my voice, and I know them, and they follow me: 28- And I give unto them eternal life; and they shall never perish, neither shall any man pluck them out of my hand. 29- My Father, which gave them me, is greater than all; and no man is able to pluck them out of my Father's hand." (John 10:27- 29)

- The Greatest Love- "For God so loved the world..." The word *world* in the Bible means:

    1) The Claw, the physical world or the earth. "In the beginning God created the heaven and the earth." (Genesis 1:1)
    2) The System or world systems. "And be not conformed to this world: but be ye transformed by the renewing

of your mind, that ye may prove what is that good, and acceptable, and perfect, will of God." (Romans 12:2)

3) The People or the humanity- everyone of all colors, nations or race. (John 3:16) God loves you and me no matter who we are and what our background is.

- The Greatest Gift- "...that he gave his only begotten Son," God gave us His only Son to die for our sins and our salvation. It could have been us who was crucified and died on the cross for our own sins, but He took all the shame and the blame. That's the reason why we celebrate holy week; it was because of what Christ did for us on the cross more than 2,000 years ago. In (Romans 5:5 "...the love of God is shed abroad in our hearts by the Holy Ghost which is given unto us." The main reason why we have comfort, peace, joy, we have the grace to live a holy life is because of the love of God... We have learned to love, to do things for God, to serve Him and learned to persevere in our sufferings and trials is because of the love of God that is shed abroad in our hearts. Do you have that love that only God can give to anyone who desire Christ? The love of God is in the Lord Jesus Christ. As you accept Him (The Lord Jesus Christ) in your heart, not only that you will have Christ in your heart but you will also have His love. "Neither is there salvation in any other: for there is none other name under heaven given among men, whereby we must be saved." (Acts 4:12)

SUNDAY
THE *ABCs* FOR ETERNAL LIFE

(I John 5-13) "These things have I written unto you that believe on the name of the Son of God; that ye may know that ye have eternal life, and that ye may believe on the name of the Son of God."

Here are some simple steps to get to heaven from where you are. It's as simple as *ABC*. The Bible is our guide on how to have eternal life in heaven.

Accept: Accept that you are a sinner. (Romans. 3:10; 23; 6:23) Accept that Jesus alone can forgive your sins and trespasses. And accept Him as your Savior and Lord of your life.

Believe: Believe on the Lord Jesus Christ as your Savior and Lord. Believe that Jesus died for your sins on the cross and he was buried and after 3 days He rose from the dead. "9- That if thou shalt confess with thy mouth the Lord Jesus, and shalt believe in thine heart that God hath raised him from the dead, thou shalt be saved." 10- For with the heart man believeth unto righteousness; and with the mouth confession is made unto salvation. 11- For the scripture saith, Whosoever believeth on him shall not be ashamed. 12- For there is no difference between the Jew and the Greek: for the same Lord over all is rich unto all that call upon him. 13- For whosoever shall call upon the name of the Lord shall be saved." (Romans 10: 9- 13) "But as many as received him, to them gave he power to become the sons of God, even to them that believe on his name:" (John 1: 12)

Confess: Confess your sins to God. You ask the Lord to forgive you of your sins and to cleanse you from all unrighteousness. "8- If we say that we have no sin, we deceive ourselves, and the truth is not in us. 9- If we confess our sins, he is faithful and just to forgive us our sins, and to cleanse us from all unrighteousness. 10- If we say that we have not sinned, we make him a liar, and his word is not in us." (I John 1: 8- 10) It's so easy to understand and do. Try Jesus today!

God will remain faithful even if we will turn our back from Him. He will not take the salvation away from anyone who sins or was lacking in some ways. He is faithful to His promises and the promised of eternal life in heaven. It's not based on our performance and attitude, but was based on what He has done at cross of Calvary. He paid it all and can't be taken back...It's not like a mortgage where you have foreclosures and the bank could take your property or take control of your business if you don't get to pay them. The sad thing about it is the bank has the right to the property or can still take the property from the owner and you lost everything you paid for years. Praise God! This will not apply to our free gift of salvation through the death of His Son. Even if we miss the mark, we committed sin (God forbid)... salvation will still be ours. Paul wrote; "8- But God commendeth his love toward us, in that, while we were yet sinners, Christ died for us. 9- Much more then, being now justified by his blood, we shall be saved from wrath through him." (Romans 5:8- 9)

MONDAY
BE GRATEFUL
(Exodus 16:1- 2) "11- And the LORD spake unto Moses, saying, 12- I have heard the murmurings of the children of Israel: speak unto them, saying, At even ye shall eat flesh, and in the morning ye shall be filled with bread; and ye shall know that I am the LORD your God."

People all over the world are complaining and murmurings just like the Israelites of old, they always complain or they always have something to complain about. Gratefulness or being thankful is very important in our daily walk with God. Being appreciative or grateful is very important as God's light in this darkened world. People have complains on almost everything. No wonder at the mall, in tourist areas, in buildings and businesses; we can see a customer service or a complain desks. We read of the Israelites complained to Moses and to God in spite of God's provision. People complain of the terrible traffic while others on the other side of the globe walk miles or just ride a bike to be able to go from point *A* to point *B*. Some of us in the United States of America are complaining of the grapes with seeds, while in some parts of the world they only have grapes on special occasions like Christmas. Are we stepping on the Israelites' of old footsteps or pattern of life or are we walking in the path of righteousness? We are in the Lord Jesus Christ's pathway. I love this hymn; "Count your blessings name them one by one... and see what the Lord has done" Be thankful to God for your family, friends and financial condition even if it's not as good as you may have expected it to be. (Psalms 100:3- 5; 105:1- 3) Be thankful to God in all things according to the most grateful man in the New Testament era. "In everything give thanks: for this is the will of God in Christ Jesus concerning you." (I Thessalonians 5: 18)

Thankfulness, gratefulness, gratitude, thank you or praise God are not the common words we say when things are not going right and well. Unfortunately, it's not a common vocabulary to many individuals and homes. We may have thousands of things to be thankful for; but we can easily be diverted to complain and concentrate on little things to complain about. But the Holy Bible said, "In everything give thanks…" Pastors and preachers must learn to teach their congregations to be grateful to God. Parents and teachers should help their children exercise "gratefulness" at all times. Let us be grateful to God for who we are, what we have and even for what we don't have. In other words; contentment and satisfaction must be in our systems. It should be in our hearts, in our mind and in our soul. During my times in the seminary at the International Baptist Theological College campus; we have Morning devotion at 5:30 AM. Before the speaker would start the sharing of the Word of God, we usually sing this beautiful song:

> "Thank you Lord for saving my soul;
> Thank you Lord for making me whole
> Thank you Lord for giving to me,
> Thy great salvation so pure and free…"

"1- Praise ye the LORD. O give thanks unto the LORD; for he is good: for his mercy endureth forever. 48- Blessed be the LORD God of Israel from everlasting to everlasting: and let all the people say, Amen. Praise ye the LORD." (Psalm 106:1; 48)

TUESDAY

MANNA – IT'S SWEET, SMALL AND WHITE.

(Exodus 16:31) "31- And the house of Israel called the name thereof Manna: and it was like coriander seed, white; and the taste of it was like wafers made with honey."

In spite of God's provision, the Israelites still complained of so many things. God the Father sent them manna which is the picture of the Lord Jesus Christ. It speaks of Christ's character. "My meditation of him shall be sweet: I will be glad in the LORD." (Psalms 104:34) Just like what the song says: "'Tis so sweet to trust in Jesus, just to take Him at His word, just to rest upon His promise, Just to know, "Thus saith the LORD…" "O taste and see that the LORD is good; blessed is the man that trusteth in him." (Psalms 34:8) The words "taste" and "see" are two important words. It means put God to the test and experience God and see how kind He is to you! It means you watch and see the way His mercies showered down on all who trust in him. To *taste* means to experience and to see for ourselves the goodness of the LORD. God wants to get into our senses. When you taste something, you also get to feel and smell. The spiritual significance of the verse is that we as Christians should take a step of faith so we can be partakers of God's goodness. (Psalms 23:5) Exercise your faith by taking Christ in His Word. You will never know unless you experience it yourself by trusting in the Lord. You will never know the goodness of God until you are there. The sweetness and the goodness of God are 2 of the things that the Israelites overlooked when they were in the wilderness. Those are 2 of the things that we took for granted as we walk through in our own wilderness. Instead of walking with God in His goodness and sweetness; we walked in bitterness of soul, complaints and we walk in the wilderness of sin and ungratefulness. God is faithful and He is faithful all the time. It means even in His judgment, we can see the Lord's faithfulness. When we say God is faithful all the time, it means even in our trials and suffering, in our pain and sorrow, in our joy and extremity and even in sickness and prosperity. When we say God is faithful, it means we refer to its entire creations and what He is doing with it. God cannot change His character as a loving and faithful God. God is faithful even in His creations- the natures. (Psalm 119:90) God's faithfulness is beyond our imaginations and comprehension. There's no word to express His faithfulness to His creations. God has provided and will continue to provide our needs. He is our Manna, sweet and wonderful Manna in life. If you just think of how the Lord provided the needs of the Israelites, it was like a "food stamp" in a form of a miracle. "Food stamp" in the USA is the help the government have been giving to the less fortunate. The Israelites did not work for it and it was free of charge given to them by the King of kings and Lord of lords. The taste of the manna was sweet- a great picture of the sweetness of the Lord in spite of their rebellion and doubt. Small is a picture of God's humility to a proud humanity. (Philippians 2:5- 10) The Psalmists wrote; "11- For the LORD God is a sun and shield: the LORD will give grace and glory: no good thing will he withhold from them that walk uprightly. 12- O LORD of hosts, blessed is the man that trusteth in thee." (Psalm 84: 11- 12)

WEDNESDAY
THE PREVALENT ATTITUDES OF MEN

(Numbers 11: 4 – 6) "4- And the mixed multitude that was among them fell a lusting: and the children of Israel also wept again, and said, who shall give us flesh to eat? 5- We remember the fish, which we did eat in Egypt freely; the cucumbers, and the melons, and the leeks, and the onions, and the garlick: 6- But now our soul is dried away: there is nothing at all, beside this manna, before our eyes."

"bdellium" is like a "droplets of gum from the bark of a tree" In (verse 5) lusting will lead to weeping, and then we complain. The next thing we do is we question God and His Word and eventually, we totally doubt God and His Word. In (verse 6) shows us the picture of a Christian whose heart and mind is still in the world of which somehow be out of focus to God. They would always think of their good dinner in Egypt and what they have when they were still in their worldly pleasures. There's something better than fish, cucumber, onions and garlic. There's something better than what the whole world can offer. We have God and if you have God, you have everything. God owns the universe. The Israelites does not have the same attitude as the Filipinos with just rice, fish and vegetables on their plates 3 times a day and it's a cycle.

The manna may have a gummy texture on it. I cannot picture to you the taste and texture of it, but I'm very much sure that the manna would not be that bad. It should be like *rice* to every Filipinos, *Potato* to Indians or Americans and may be *shawarma* to the Arabic. The Israelites did not appreciate the manna from God because their hearts were still in Egypt. This is the prevalent attitude of man. Nothing has changed; even the technology, medical and science was already been there. (Acts 12: 10; Genesis 2:22- 24; Genesis 28:10- 14)

The Israelites during the time of Moses cannot feel the sweetness of the Lord in their prayers, Bible study and worship; because their heart is still in the world, it's in Egypt.

The 7 Prevalent Attitudes of Men are:

1- We complain in good times, to the good and better things.
2- We are dissatisfied with everything.
3- We have no contentment.
4- We gossip and criticize others for our own satisfaction.
5- We want to have more and we become selfish.
6- We have superiority complex and sometimes we don't look at the needs of other people.
7- We are very ungrateful to God, to the leadership and to other people.

Apostle Paul said; "11- Not that I speak in respect of want: for I have learned, in whatsoever state I am, therewith to be content." (Philippians 4:11)

THURSDAY

"WHY LOVE, JESTING AND GOSSIP CAN'T BE IN ONE ROOM?"

(Ephesians 5:3- 4) "3- But fornication, and all uncleanness, or covetousness, let it not be once named among you, as becometh saints;4- Neither filthiness, nor foolish talking, nor jesting, which are not convenient: but rather giving of thanks."

We all like to have fun and enjoy every minute of our lives here on earth; but there are times and there are things that we, as Christians needs to draw a line or make a boundary. What is "Jesting" anyways? According to Dictionary.com; "Jesting" means "a joke or witty remark; witticism. 2. a bantering remark; a piece of good-natured ridicule; taunt. 3. sport or fun: *to speak half in jest, half in earnest*. 4. The object of laughter, sport, or mockery; laughing-stock. Some of the "stand up" comedians are using the Bible, the name of God, hell, calamities and spiritual matters as their subjects for their jokes. It's very ungodly, it's sarcasm and it's a sacrilege. Here are some of the Scripture references with regards to foolish talking, foolishness or bad jokes, green jokes or dirty jokes. "23- It is as sport to a fool to do mischief: but a man of understanding hath wisdom. 32- The lips of the righteous know what is acceptable: but the mouth of the wicked speaketh frowardness [NKJV: what is perverse]. 9- Fools make a mock at sin: but among the righteous there is favour. 21- Folly is joy to him that is destitute of wisdom: but a man of understanding walketh uprightly. 18- As a mad man who casteth firebrands, arrows, and death, 19- So is the man that deceiveth his neighbor and saith, Am not I in sport?" (Proverbs 10:23, 32; 14:9; 15:21; 26:18- 19) You cannot put love, gossip and jesting in one room. (I John 3:15) You cannot reconcile love and bitterness without the blood of the Lord Jesus Christ. And you cannot reconcile love and hatred without forgiveness standing in the middle. It's impossible to reconcile the Bible to false teachings, religions, beliefs and what the world believed in and practiced? The Bible is opposite from the enemy's path. We need *to love God* and *love our neighbors* as ourselves. *"Hereby perceive we the love of God, because he laid down his life for us: and we ought to lay down our lives for the brethren." (I John 3:16)* Mohandas Gandhi said; "Where there is love there is life..." We perceive (we discern, we observe) or we have witnessed the love of God. How? "...because he laid down His life for us." It was God the Father who manifested His love to us through the death of His Son- the Lord Jesus Christ. This is the proof of God's love. Leo Buscaglia said; "Love is life... And if you miss love, you miss life." God has set an example for us to follow. It is God's character to love and He wants for us to love one another and not hate each other. We were made in God's image and not in the image of the animals so we can bite and eliminate each other or destroy one another. "26- And God said, Let us make man in our image, after our likeness: and let them have dominion over the fish of the sea, and over the fowl of the air, and over the cattle, and over all the earth, and over every creeping thing that creepeth upon the earth. 27- So God created man in his own image, in the image of God created he him; male and female created he them." (Genesis 1:26- 27)

FRIDAY

VIP- Very Important Person

(Thessalonians 1:11-12) "11- Wherefore also we pray always for you, that our God would count you worthy of this calling, and fulfill all the good pleasure of his goodness, and the work of faith with power: 12-That the name of our Lord Jesus Christ may be glorified in you, and ye in him, according to the grace of our God and the Lord Jesus Christ."

According to Matthew Henry: "...that God would carry on the good work that is begun, and fulfill all the good pleasure of his goodness... The good pleasure of God denotes his gracious purposes towards his people, which flow from his goodness, and are full of goodness towards them; and it is thence that all good comes to us. If there be any good in us, it is the fruit of God's good-will to us, it is owing to the good pleasure of his goodness, and therefore is called grace." (The Bible Collection, Suite) Life is full of surprises. Millions of people are living with no direction and millions are living one day at a time. But the sad part is millions of lives are like what the song says..."Que sera, sera, whatever will be, will be..." We want to be treated like a VIP (Very Important Person). We want to have a special treatment. We want to be on the top of every situation. We can always look back to what He has done in the past and give Him the glory for all the things that God has done for you. It's for Him and all because of Him anyways. Whatever God has done for us, He did it and will continue to do it because of His love for us. He wants to get the glory He deserved. It is for God and God alone... We sometimes wanted to take control of everything. People want to be in control of their finances and life, but we don't know the avenue to success and how to make it to the top. There are important things that we need to have in making our way to true blessings. Of course, we need to have the Lord Jesus Christ. (John 1:12) We need to live our lives according to God's purpose and will. We are *Valuable to God*. It doesn't matter who you are, where you are, what your background is. God loves you and you are of more value than the lilies in the field and the whole world. Jesus said; "For what shall it profit a man, if he shall gain the whole world, and lose his own soul?" Be *Involved in Christ*. (John 17:7- 8) We don't need a lottery and big chunk of money to be called prosperous; we need the Lord Jesus Christ. "And if children, then heirs; heirs of God, and joint-heirs with Christ; if so be that we suffer with him, that we may be also glorified together." (Roman 8:17) We want to be counted worthy of His calling, whatever we may have from God. I'm not talking about preaching and missions, but anything God is leading you to do for His name and glory. God's grace and goodness will be with us. If God is leading us and using us in His field, let us be counted worthy for His glory. God is our VIP. He is more important than anything and to anyone in this life. "I therefore, the prisoner of the Lord, beseech you that ye walk worthy of the vocation wherewith ye are called," (Ephesians 4:1)

SATURDAY
WE NEED VISION
(Proverbs 29:18) "18- Where there is no vision, the people perish: but he that keepeth the law, happy is he."

The world calls it *ambition but to some it's a vision*. It's very sad to know and to see that millions of people don't have vision or ambition in life. Oh, it's not just the people from the third world countries, but people of all race and cultures. They are wasting so much time by just being idle, servants of a small thing called games both in computer and television. Some have lost so much time and money in gambling. If you have an *ambition*, you will also take some actions. You will never get to your destination by just standing around the corner or by playing games and doing nothing. You won't make it to the top by just looking at the ladder. You can't cross the ocean by just standing on the port or pier. You have to get on the boat or ship. You can't fly to your destination by just wondering how this huge steel could fly up to 30,000 feet. You have to do something; you get on the plane, trust the plane and the pilot. Together with your ambition and action would be your *aim*. Others call it goal or focus. Try to have a goal and stay focus. When you play the archery or lawn tennis, *focus* is so important. One of the reasons that destroys the game and momentum of an athlete is when they start to stay out of focus. I was at the church planter's seminar of the Southern Baptist Convention and I enjoy it. Rev. Chris McNairy was the speaker. He is from the North American Mission Board. I'm so honored to know this man of God for quite a while. Rev. McNairy shared to us about the *Principle of Vision* from the book of (Habakkuk 2:1-4). In the book of Joshua chapter one; God the Father wanted Joshua to re-focus his heart and mind after he got destructed by the death of Moses. Joshua was probably so down, stressed out or depressed, because of the death of his leader and mentor- Moses, the servant of God. (Joshua 1:1- 5)

Check the 20/20 Spiritual Vision: 1) Watch, 2) Write, 3) Work; 4) Wait- *"Where there is no vision, the people perish: but he that keepeth the law, happy is he."* (Proverbs 29:18) We need to *watch* both our physical and spiritual life. Watch your diet, watch your weight, watch your heart and watch what you're eating. We need to watch our spiritual life and our enemy- the devil. The Bible says; "1- I will stand upon my watch, and set me upon the tower, and will watch to see what he will say unto me, and what I shall answer when I am reproved. 8-Be sober, be vigilant; because your adversary the devil, as a roaring lion, walketh about, seeking whom he may devour." (Habakkuk 2:1; I Peter 5:8) You need to write whatever vision, dreams, and goals that you may have in mind and place it somewhere that is visible for you to see. "And the LORD answered me, and said, Write the vision, and make it plain upon tables, that he may run that readeth it." (Habakkuk 2:2) *We need to work* and work hard for God. Laziness is a brother of foolishness. We expect God to work in us and through us, but if we don't even lift our finger for Jesus, I believe we have a wrong expectation. "Behold ye among the heathen, and regard, and wonder marvellously: for I will work a work in your days, which ye will not believe, though it be told you." (Habakkuk 1:5) *We need to wait* and wait patiently. I honestly don't like waiting and I believe that millions will agree with me because you went through the same problem- *wait patiently.* Isaiah wrote; "29- He giveth power to the faint; and to them that have no might he increaseth strength.30- Even the youths shall faint and be weary, and the young men shall utterly fall: 31- But they that wait upon the LORD shall renew their strength; they shall mount up with wings as eagles; they shall run, and not be weary; and they shall walk, and not faint." (Isaiah 40:29- 31)

SUNDAY
YOU NEED DETERMINATION AND INSPIRATION

(Hebrews 12:1-2) "1- Wherefore seeing we also are compassed about with so great a cloud of witnesses, let us lay aside every weight, and the sin which doth so easily beset us, and let us run with patience the race that is set before us, 2- Looking unto Jesus the author and finisher of our faith; who for the joy that was set before him endured the cross, despising the shame, and is set down at the right hand of the throne of God."

The good example of determination is in the life and death of the Lord Jesus Christ. Christ gave made a sacrificed for our sins. Millions of people have watched the movie "The Passion of the Christ"; how the Lord Jesus Christ endured the cross...! He despised the shame... although the movie did not picture the true suffering of the Lord Jesus Christ as recorded in the Bible. He is the Son of God but Christ was willing to humble Himself, take up the cross and follow and obey God the Father for the forgiveness of our sins. Jesus should be the Christian's inspiration in every step of the way. *Inspiration-* We need inspiration from the Lord and the Holy Spirit. "But the Comforter, which is the Holy Ghost, whom the Father will send in my name, he shall teach you all things, and bring all things to your remembrance, whatsoever I have said unto you." (John 14:26); "But when the Comforter is come, whom I will send unto you from the Father, even the Spirit of truth, which proceedeth from the Father, he shall testify of me." (John 15:26) We should be inspired by the Holy Spirit of God. (Philippians 3:13- 14) Notice these people who made it as they exercised their faith along with their determination and inspiration to do things for our Lord and for His honor and glory. It requires endurance and focus as well for you to make it. In (Hebrews 11:29- 31) We can see the Lord's provision in times of difficulties and He used the unexpected person and resources to provide what they needed and when they needed them; verse "31- By faith the harlot Rahab perished not with them that believed not". Mr. Derek Redmond was a great athlete who very well represented his country with pride and honor. He was a man of determination and a man who is also an inspiration to many young people. He showed the whole world during the Barcelona Olympics when his hamstring snapped during the semi- finals by his dedication and love for his team and for his country by being focused in spite of pain and uncomfortable circumstances. As one of Britain's greatest ever 400m Olympic athletes, Derek have set an example for us to follow; not just in sport but in our daily walk. In Derek's web page, it says; "No matter how meticulous the preparation, how dedicated the team and the individual, life has a habit of delivering the unexpected. When that happens it is vital to stay focused, adjust objectives and goals as necessary and maintain the drive for success." (Internet at Yahoo- Derek Redmond Webpage) Determination and inspiration are inseparable. Mr. Derek was determined and alongside with him was his dad who inspired him. We get our inspiration from the Lord and along with God's inspiration must be our determination. Apostle Paul wrote; (I 24- "24-Know ye not that they which run in a race run all, but one receiveth the prize? So run, that ye may obtain. 25- And every man that striveth for the mastery is temperate in all things. Now they do it to obtain a corruptible crown; but we an incorruptible. 26- I therefore so run, not as uncertainly; so fight I, not as one that beateth the air: 27- But I keep under my body, and bring it into subjection: lest that by any means, when I have preached to others, I myself should be a castaway." Corinthians 9:24- 27)

MONDAY
BE INSPIRED!

(Habakkuk 2:1-3) "1- I will stand upon my watch, and set me upon the tower, and will watch to see what he will say unto me, and what I shall answer when I am reproved. 2- And the LORD answered me, and said, Write the vision, and make it plain upon tables, that he may run that readeth it. 3- For the vision is yet for an appointed time, but at the end it shall speak, and not lie: though it tarry, wait for it; because it will surely come, it will not tarry."

We need inspiration from the Word of God. The book of Psalms and the book of John are one of the books from the Bible that I read when I get discouraged or just want to be encouraged. We need to read our Bible. We need inspiration from the pastors. Pastors should watch their words and comments when talking to their members. Pastors, church leaders or parents can either be an encouragement and an inspiration or be the cause of discouragement or downfall of an individual. "Ointment and perfume rejoice the heart: so doth the sweetness of a man's friend by hearty counsel." (Proverbs 27:9) Be inspired by the life of the servants of God. Be inspired by the life and dedication of the missionaries all over the world. Be inspired of what God is doing in the life of His people. Be inspired by the service of His servants in the field. By those whose life is dedicated to the work of the Lord. By those who have given their lives for the cause of Christ. Be inspired by the life of those who follow or followed the Lord in many ways and in spite of the odd in life. There are those who have served God in the midst of extremity or financial difficulties. Remember the pastors and the missionaries who made it in the ministry in spite of the pain and difficulties in life. Remember your fellow believers whose life became an inspiration for you to go on. We need inspiration from the successful world athletes and businessmen. I've read some books about athletes and businessmen and women who made it to the top. And be inspired of what Christ has done for us and the dedication of the prophets, disciples, and servants of God.

Karate Kid is a good movie about determination, inspiration, partnership and encouragement. WWJD- What Would Jesus Do is another Christian movie that will really inspire you with how they stood together to save their church from the local government's plan of turning it into a casino, because the church were not able to pay their mortgage for a few months. They were inspired and convicted by the strangers' words of encouragement and short sermon to them which leads them to stand together for the Lord and for their church. They even stood with their pastor in his depression due to the death of his wife and son in a car accident. Your unpleasant circumstances and people's negative attitudes towards you should not be the cause to pull you down to the lowest level of your life. But that should inspire you to do more and to excel to the top and prosper. Here in these verses, we have the inspiration from Jethro; "9- And Jethro rejoiced for all the goodness which the LORD had done to Israel, whom he had delivered out of the hand of the Egyptians. 10- And Jethro said, blessed be the LORD, who hath delivered you out of the hand of the Egyptians, and out of the hand of Pharaoh, who hath delivered the people from under the hand of the Egyptians." (Exodus 18:9- 10)

TUESDAY
WE NEED PASSION

(James 5:17) "Elias was a man subject to like passions as we are, and he prayed earnestly that it might not rain: and it rained not on the earth by the space of three years and six months."

The Passion of God's people in the Bible:

- To Abraham, passion is when he obeyed the Lord's voice to sacrifice his son Isaac in mount Moriah. "1- And it came to pass after these things, that God did tempt Abraham, and said unto him, Abraham: and he said, Behold, here I am. 2- And he said, Take now thy son, thine only son Isaac, whom thou lovest, and get thee into the land of Moriah; and offer him there for a burnt offering upon one of the mountains which I will tell thee of." (Genesis 22:1- 2)

- To Daniel, it was his desire to pray and to stand for the truth and to be a testimony in the kingdom. "8- But Daniel purposed in his heart that he would not defile himself with the portion of the king's meat, nor with the wine which he drank: therefore he requested of the prince of the eunuchs that he might not defile himself." 17- "As for these four children, God gave them knowledge and skill in all learning and wisdom: and Daniel had understanding in all visions and dreams." (Daniel 1:8; 17)

- To Paul, his passion was to be a witness to the Jew first and also to the Greeks. We can see Paul's passion in his letter in the book of Romans, he wrote; "For I am not ashamed of the gospel of Christ: for it is the power of God unto salvation to ever one that believeth; to the Jew first, and also to the Greek." (Romans 1:16)

- To David, his passion was to kill the bears, the lions and the giant Goliath. His passion was to do the cause of God. David said in (I Samuel 17:29) "Is there not a cause?" David's passion was his desire to do the cause of God and for God. His passion was to bring honor in the name of God by killing the giant Goliath who defies God.

Hebbel the German poet and dramatist said; "Nothing great in the world has ever been accomplished without passion." (Hebbel quotes, German poet and dramatist- 1813-1863)

Mitch Albom said; "The way you get meaning into your life is to devote yourself to loving others, devote yourself to your community around you, and devote yourself to creating something that gives you purpose and meaning."

Oscar Wilde said; "Between men and women there is no friendship possible. There is passion, enmity, worship, love, but no friendship." (Oscar Wilde, Irish Poet, Novelist, Dramatist and Critic- 1854-1900) – Yahoo, Thinkexist.com) Those are interesting quotes from people who have passion in life and we should live a life with at least passion for God, for people or something. As a pastor, I have my own personal passion. My passion is to see people coming to know Christ as their Lord and Savior. My passion is to see His church grow in the Lord and in numbers. My passion is to see our youth being passionate in music, in the Word of God, in the ministry and in mission. My passion for my family was for them to get saved, to know the Lord as their Savior. And I rejoice for EJ coming to know the Lord last October 22, 2008. What is your passion or do you have a passion for God? We exercise our passion, knowing that there will be ups and down. Your passion must come with compassion. The Bible says; "And of some have compassion, making a difference:" (Jude 1:22)

WEDNESDAY
VIP- VISION, INSPIRATION, PASSION

(Proverbs 29:18) "Where there is no vision, the people perish: but he that keepeth the law, happy is he."

I shared to my children about *passion* and I told them that if they really have passion for music; you will eat, sleep, drink, drive and dream about it. It means you will see it in your food, in your pillows, in your wheel while you're driving and you can go on and on... Notice here what Matthew Henry said about his commentary on (Hosea 4:6) "Hosea My people are destroyed for lack of knowledge: because thou hast rejected knowledge, I will also reject thee, that thou shalt be no priest to me: seeing thou hast forgotten the law of thy God, I will also forget thy children." "See what reason we have to be thankful to God for the plenty of open vision which we enjoy. II. The felicity of a people that have not only a settled, but a successful ministry among them, the people that hear and keep the law, among whom religion is uppermost; happy are such a people and every particular person among them. It is not having the law, but obeying it, and living up to it, that will entitle us to blessedness." "24- Though he fall, he shall not be utterly cast down: for the LORD upholdeth him with his hand. 37- Mark the perfect man, and behold the upright: for the end of that man is peace." (Psalm 37:24, 37) The Lord has given us the grace to serve Him and along with His unlimited grace should be our vision, inspiration and passion for Him and the lost world as we win them for Christ. (Philippians 2:12- 14; Habakkuk 2: 1- 3)

I recently was talking to a pastor about vision and passion. I told him that when you have passion and vision I said; for me, it means you're going to sleep, eat and work hard to make it happen. So many pastors and leaders will just go through the flow in the ministry without even realizing that they need to have passion and be passionate with what they're doing for the Lord. I was surprise to meet with pastors about a big concert that I was planning and proposing to them. I was inviting an international artist to do a concert in their province that would not cost them a single cent. And they all refused the offer for so many negative reasons. But I can put their negative remarks and reasoning in 5 words- "lack of passion and vision". Sometimes people need a little push to start something significant. We need to push and make our children and some of our friends see the big picture. If you're a pastor or a leader, you must be a visionary, an inspiration and you must have the passion for people and in what you are doing for the Lord. Leaders must have the passion to make things happen. You can't be a good pastor or leader unless you have the VIP- Vision, Inspiration and Passion. And success would not be possible if you don't exercise and put VIP into practice and live a life with Vision, Inspiration and Passion. King Solomon was a man of vision, he wrote; "He also that is slothful in his work is brother to him that is a great waster." "Where there is no vision, the people perish: but he that keepeth the law, happy is he." (Proverbs 18:9; 29:18)

THURSDAY
PETER, THE WOUNDED SOLDIER OF GOD

(Matthew 16:13- 18) "13- When Jesus came into the coasts of Caesarea Philippi, he asked his disciples, saying, Whom do men say that I the Son of man am? 14- And they said, Some say that thou art John the Baptist: some, Elias; and others, Jeremias, or one of the prophets. 15- He saith unto them, But whom say ye that I am? 16- And Simon Peter answered and said, Thou art the Christ, the Son of the living God. 17- And Jesus answered and said unto him, Blessed art thou, Simon Barjona: for flesh and blood hath not revealed it unto thee, but my Father which is in heaven. 18- And I say also unto thee, That thou art Peter, and upon this rock I will build my church; and the gates of hell shall not prevail against it."

Peter declared the Deity of the Lord Jesus Christ. We can talk about Peter weaknesses and sins. We can talk about his denial of our Lord and how he lived in carnality and worldly pleasures. Sometimes people would just look at your fault, mistakes, sins, your downfall and negative things in you and just overlooked the good things in you. (I Peter 3:18) Let's look at the positive things that happened to Peter. Peter was a wounded soldier who was restored by the Lord in His grace. What do you do when your brother fails? What do you do when your brother is wounded? We must learn to minister to our wounded soldier. We must learn to encourage our wounded brothers and sisters. The Lord did not condemn Peter when he sinned and failed. When you do things for God, people sometimes will have something to say either positive or negative. They will look on the negative side of life. Peter failed the Lord, but God restored him. I have friends and pastors who were wounded and were devastated due to temptation, because of money issues and financial difficulties, moral issues and others because of doctrinal issues. We can be judgmental or we may just close our eyes like nothing happens. But we cannot deny the fact that people are hurting, but the irony… some Christians don't even feel it or may pretend like they don't see it. People are suffering from the wound and from the dart of Satan.

We must focus our attention in the Lord Jesus Christ. This is one of the positive sides of Peter when he confessed Jesus' Deity. It means that Peter confessed the Lord Jesus Christ as the Son of God and God Himself. We must be aware of the false teaching about Christ and His Deity, because this is very important and a major doctrine in the Bible. The Jews recognized Jesus as an individual who did something significant for the people, but they don't accept His Lordship and as the coming Messiah. They don't accept Him as the Christ, the Son of the living God and the second person of the holy trinity. The religious groups that are not Christians have the same belief. They don't believe in the Lord Jesus Christ except He was a plain man. Apostle Paul wrote; "5- Let this mind be in you, which was also in Christ Jesus: 6- Who, being in the form of God, thought it not robbery to be equal with God:7- But made himself of no reputation, and took upon him the form of a servant, and was made in the likeness of men: 8- And being found in fashion as a man, he humbled himself, and became obedient unto death, even the death of the cross. 9- "Wherefore God also hath highly exalted him, and given him a name which is above every name: 10- That at the name of Jesus every knee should bow, of things in heaven, and things in earth, and things under the earth;" (Philippians 2: 5- 10)

FRIDAY
GOD'S GENEROSITY= LOVE

(I John 4:7-8) "7- Beloved, let us love one another: for love is of God; and every one that loveth is born of God, and knoweth God. 8- He that loveth not knoweth not God; for God is love."

Love, I believe is God's greatest nature. God loves us in spite of our sinfulness. God did not look at us as a thing to love. God look at us as a human being, although we're unworthy of His great love, yet He loves us unconditionally. He could have loved the universe and its beauty or He could have loved the deepest depth of the ocean and its beauty, yet God choose to love us. He even could have loved His other creations like the animals and natures, but God choose to love us. And because of His great love for us, He gave us His only begotten Son. "For God so loved the world, that he gave his only begotten Son, that whosoever believeth in him should not perish, but have everlasting life." (John 3:16)

Jesus the Son of God gave His life for us. "9- As the Father hath loved me, so have I loved you: continue ye in my love. If ye keep my commandments, ye shall abide in my love; even as I have kept my Father's commandments, and abide in his love." (John 15:9-10)

God the Father showed us His love through the Lord Jesus Christ. It was not a cheap kind of love like what we see and heard in Hollywood or in the movie. It costs God the Father His one and only Son. And it was not a cheap cause for Christ, because it did not only cost Him His life, but He also suffered that no man has ever went through. Every holy week; may we all ponder upon His death, burial and resurrection! Our whole being is in the hands of God the Father and in the Lord Jesus Christ and is sealed by the Holy Spirit of God until the day of redemption, It means until that day when we see Him face to face. What a glory that will be. (I Thessalonians 5:23- 24) You have heard His voice when you responded to His call for you to come to Him and follow Him for your salvation. If you did that, you are therefore with no doubt the son of the living God. What comes along with that is the promised of eternal life in heaven that cannot be taken away from you by sin, Satan and the world system. We have seen people and friends who are so generous and helpful, but no one can compare to God's generosity to every human being. The Lord created us all and along with the life that He has given us; God gave us the bonuses that we don't even deserve to have and to enjoy. We enjoy this life and the beauty of it. We enjoy the amazing beauty of God's creations. We enjoy the food, the Word of God and our relationship with Him. If you will come to Him in humility and accept the greatest gift of all- The Lord Jesus Christ and His free gift of salvation which is eternal life in heaven. That cannot be compared to any gift and to any generosity even before creation! "17- For God sent not his Son into the world to condemn the world; but that the world through him might be saved. (John 3:17)

SATURDAY
GOD'S FORGIVENESS

(Hebrews 10:4- 6) "4- For it is not possible that the blood of bulls and of goats should take away sins. 5- Wherefore when he cometh into the world, he saith, Sacrifice and offering thou wouldest not, but a body hast thou prepared me: 6- In burnt offerings and sacrifices for sin thou hast had no pleasure."

God Himself appointed Christ to the task that no one can do and to be the sacrificed. We don't need to work and work hard to go to heaven. The only reason why Christ doesn't need our religion and religious ritual is because Christ is our religion. That's the reason why we will not weight our goodness versus our badness. Christ will weight good versus evil in us by His holiness in which we all have come short of His glory. (Romans 3:10; 23) Christ is the supreme good and the only good. He is holy and He is the King of kings.

Christ reconciled us to God by His death on the Cross. "Wherefore in all things it behooved him to be made like unto his brethren, that he might be a merciful and faithful high priest in things pertaining to God, to make reconciliation for the sins of the people." (Hebrews 2:17) Paul knew he was God's enemy before his conversion, he wrote; "For if, when we were enemies, we were reconciled to God by the death of his Son, much more, being reconciled, we shall be saved by his life." (Romans 5:10) I recently was talking to a friend about forgiveness. (II Corinthians 5:18-20) We all got offended either by friends or love ones or by a stranger. We were hurt by their comments, remarks, criticism, gossip, unpleasant words and sometimes by their wrong attitudes. But the question would be; are we willing to forgive? In the movie, WWJD "What Would Jesus Do" It shows forgiveness on the part of the pastor who can't forgive himself of what happened to his family in a car accident of which he lost his wife and son. And it's also a good movie about forgiveness and being open to forgive when it shows how both church members forget the past sins and oppression. You need to take a step of faith and humble yourselves in the name of the Lord Jesus Christ. (Galatians 1:4; Ephesians 1:7) The Scripture says; "The Lord is not slack concerning his promise, as some men count slackness; but is longsuffering to us-ward, not willing that any should perish, but that all should come to repentance." (II Peter 2:9) When I was a new believer, I wrote a song from the book of Acts 3:19 and Acts 8:22; "Repent ye therefore, and be converted, that your sins may be blotted out, when the times of refreshing shall come from the presence of the Lord; Repent therefore of this thy wickedness, and pray God, if perhaps the thought of thine heart may be forgiven thee." Repentance and forgiveness- they're like train; they always come together.

Apostle Paul said it well in the book of Romans, he said; "6- For when we were yet without strength, in due time Christ died for the ungodly. 7- For scarcely for a righteous man will one die: yet peradventure for a good man some would even dare to die. 8-But God commendeth his love toward us, in that, while we were yet sinners, Christ died for us." (Romans 5:6- 8)

SUNDAY
THE DEITY OF THE LORD JESUS CHRIST
(John 17:3) "3- And this is life eternal, that they might know thee the only true God, and Jesus Christ, whom thou hast sent."

According to Wikipedia in the internet on "*Iglesia ni Cristo* beliefs of God the Father, Jesus Christ and the Holy Spirit, The Iglesia ni Cristo believes that God the Father is the only true God. The church believes that God is Omnipotent and that He created all, including Jesus Christ, the Son. Meanwhile, the Holy Spirit is the power sent by God in the name of Jesus. The Holy Spirit is in the INC ministers giving them the exclusive ability to interpret the Bible correctly. Thus, the INC rejects the trinity as a heresy. They believe that this position is attested by Jesus Christ and the Apostles. The church believes that Jesus Christ is the mediator between God the Father and humanity,[21] and was created by God the Father. God sanctified him to be without sin, and bestowed him the titles "Lord" and "Son of God". The church sees Jesus as God's highest creation, and denies his divinity. Thus, INC theology is classified as Arian by Robin A. Brace, a Britishapologist, and Anne C. Harper, former director of publications of Gordon College in Massachusetts, United States. [3] Adherents profess Jesus' substitutionary role in the redemption of humankind. He is believed to have been "foreordained before the foundation of the world", and sent by God "to deal with sin". Members "are saved by Christ's blood" who died because of his "self-sacrificing love".[2][42](From Wikipedia, the free encyclopedia) The *Iglesia ni cristo* beliefs about the trinity and the deity of the Lord Jesus Christ are questionable and not Biblical.

Jesus was from Heaven and He came down on earth. What a beautiful message- (John 3:13- 17); verse 13 "…but he that came down from heaven…" It shows that He has control of everything and as human being; there's no way we can come down from heaven once you're up there without the Lord's intervention. And there's no way a person can get out of hell without the Lord's hand. The Lord Jesus Christ was pictured in the Old Testament through the life of Joseph. If you will examine the life of Joseph in the Old Testament; it's very clear that Joseph was Jacob's beloved son. Notice here Joseph as the *son:* He was beloved of a Father. "3- Now Israel loved Joseph more than all his children, because he was the son of his old age: and he made him a coat of many colours." (John 3:16; Genesis 37:3; Hebrews 5:4- 5) Compare those verses with (Matthew 3:17). Before God the Father talked about Jesus as His beloved Son in the New Testament; He was already talking about Him (Jesus) in the Old Testament through Joseph's life. We can see Jesus in the life of Joseph and the evils that he went through by the evil plots of his selfish brothers. We can see Jesus in the life of Joseph through his sufferings and in his darkest moments and even in his betrayal. He was betrayed by his own brothers when they sold him to the merchants. Jesus was betrayed by Judas and was sold by Judas for 30 pieces of silver. And we can read and see the life of the Lord Jesus Christ in the Old Testament as pictured in the life of the prophets, kings and other symbols. It's just so amazing how God put the Bible together with Jesus His Son as the center of it. Can you make Jesus as the center of your life? The center of the Old and the New Testaments is the Lord Jesus Christ. Jesus said; "I am Alpha and Omega, the beginning and the ending, saith the Lord, which is, and which was, and which is to come, the Almighty." (Revelation 1:8)

MONDAY
JOSEPH AS A SHEPHERD

(John 10:1) "Verily, verily, I say unto you, He that entereth not by the door into the sheepfold, but climbeth up some other way, the same is a thief and a robber."

David's life is a picture of the Lord's life in the Old Testament. David was a shepherd but he called the Lord his good Shepherd… We have the Shepherd walking and leading us to His way, His will, His work and His Word. Jesus is the good Shepherd who will walk with us in the valley of the shadow of death, even in death itself. He was the *Good Shepherd* who was guiding him in his fight against the giant Goliath. (Genesis 37:2; John 10:11-14) I made a simple preaching outline about the life of Joseph from the book of Genesis. I believe that this can be beneficial to many pastors and preachers. Notice the development or progress in Joseph's life:

- In (Genesis 37:13- 14) - *Joseph as Jacob's Personal Messenger.* Verses 13- 14; "And Israel said unto Joseph, Do not thy brethren feed the flock in Shechem? come, and I will send thee unto them. And he said to him, Here am I. 14- And he said to him, Go, I pray thee, see whether it be well with thy brethren, and well with the flocks; and bring me word again. So he sent him out of the vale of Hebron, and he came to Shechem."

- In (Genesis 37:18- 20) - *The Persecution and the Plot Against Joseph by his Brothers.* Verses 18; "And when they saw him afar off, even before he came near unto them, they conspired against him to slay him. 19- And they said one to another, Behold, this dreamer cometh. 20- Come now therefore, and let us slay him, and cast him into some pit, and we will say, Some evil beast hath devoured him: and we shall see what will become of his dreams."

- In (Genesis 37:22- 24) - *Joseph was Cast Down into the Pit by his Envious Brothers.* Verse 22- 24; "And Reuben said unto them, Shed no blood, but cast him into this pit that is in the wilderness, and lay no hand upon him; that he might rid him out of their hands, to deliver him to his father again. 23- And it came to pass, when Joseph was come unto his brethren, that they stripped Joseph out of his coat, his coat of many colours that was on him; 24- And they took him, and cast him into a pit: and the pit was empty, there was no water in it."

- In (Genesis 37:26- 27) - *Joseph was Sold for Profit by His Greedy Brothers.* Verses 26; "And Judah said unto his brethren, what profit is it if we slay our brother, and conceal his blood? 27- Come, and let us sell him to the Ishmeelites, and let not our hand be upon him; for he is our brother and our flesh. And his brethren were content."

- In (Genesis 39:1) — *Joseph was Under the Authority and Power of Potiphar.* Verse 1; "Come, and let us sell him to the Ishmeelites, and let not our hand be upon him; for he is our brother and our flesh. And his brethren were content."

- In (Genesis 39:20) - *Joseph was Put in Prison Because of False Accusation.* Verse 20; "And Joseph's master took him, and put him into the prison, a place where the king's prisoners were bound: and he was there in the prison."

- *He is the Good Shepherd who Helped Joseph as he Made the Right Decision on His Way from Pit to Become the Prime Minister of Egypt.* Jesus is your *good Shepherd* when you were in your deepest moment and when you're in need of wisdom and guidance. Would you trust the Shepherd of your soul? Jesus said; "I am the door: by me if any man enter in, he shall be saved, and shall go in and out, and find pasture." (John 10:9)

TUESDAY

ARE YOU IN BONDAGE?

(Exodus 2:23- 25) "23- And it came to pass in process of time, that the king of Egypt died: and the children of Israel sighed by reason of the bondage, and they cried, and their cry came up unto God by reason of the bondage. 24- And God heard their groaning, and God remembered his covenant with Abraham, with Isaac, and with Jacob. 25- And God looked upon the children of Israel, and God had respect unto them."

The Philippines was under the power and authority of the Spaniards from 1514- 1898, only after the USA government support and helped the Philippines gained its independence. It was just after the US- Spanish war that the Philippines were freed from being in bondage. We have similar scenarios happening in many countries in some parts of the world right now. And the same scenarios that are happening in many homes, in many hearts and in many heads or minds of some individuals. They are real homes, real hearts and real minds that are struggling right now, because they're in bondage. Some of them knew that they are in bondage, others they just ignore it, while to some it's just a part of life. Those who are in bondage; it's just something that they have to live by every minute of an hour, every hour of the day and every days of the week. It's sad, but unless you will *do* something about it, you will never get out of it and be free. I shared something very private to a friend one day, and he said something with an accent; "Ely, it will not gonna happen!!!" That's what others thought before they were really in bondage and can't get out of it anymore. The Philippines would never be free from the Spanish injustices, oppressions and rules, if the USA government and some of the Filipino heroes did not do something and stood up against the Spaniards. I remember a story of a pastor friend about the prisoner who was kept in a very small place and he was seated almost all the time. And when he was freed, he can't stand and walk because he lost his balance being used in a seated position for a long time. It's just so sad that millions of people all over the world are in the same situations spiritually. Billions of people are in the same situations in terms of their spiritual condition before God. They're lost and they're servants of sin and of Satan and they don't even know it. I'm proud to have a Spanish blood. My mom and my dad's parents were from Spain. But, I'm thankful to God for the freedom in our country, because someone fought and died for it. The book of John has all the information about satisfaction, how to be free from bondage and about the love of God, the Deity of the Lord Jesus Christ and so much more... A friend of mine said; "Someone made a bad decision which leads to his imprisonment... This guy has been in bondage with such sin for a long time and he did not even realize it..." I replied; "You see he is out there and we're thinking that this guy is a free man, but he is in prison of his own sin and weaknesses. So, now he is in prison because of the sin which he has been in bondage of... and a prisoner for his sin." The Bible said; "32- And ye shall know the truth, and the truth shall make you free. 33- They answered him, We be Abraham's seed, and were never in bondage to any man: how sayest thou, Ye shall be made free? 34- Jesus answered them, Verily, verily, I say unto you, Whosoever committeth sin is the servant of sin." 37- "All that the Father giveth me shall come to me; and him that cometh to me I will in no wise cast out." (John 8: 32- 34; 6:37)

WEDNESDAY

THE REASONS FOR THEIR BURDENS…

(Exodus 2:11-12) "11- And it came to pass in those days, when Moses was grown, that he went out unto his brethren, and looked on their burdens: and he spied an Egyptian smiting an Hebrew, one of his brethren. 12- And he looked this way and that way, and when he saw that there was no man, he slew the Egyptian, and hid him in the sand."

Some Christians can come and go to church not as servants, but as individuals who are just doing the rituals and as a plain listener. You can be a Christian and still be in bondage of something sinful. No one can ever be a servant unless he decides to be one. To be a servant and to be in bondage is a matter of choice. And there are those who made a choice to be in bondage and don't even know it. Moses in this text is a picture of the Lord Jesus Christ. The Israelites were in bondage. Why were they in bondage? The reason for their burdens and being in bondage was because of the works of the devil. Satan will give us the burden both bad and evil. (Exodus 2:11) King Pharaoh is a picture of Satan in this story. This is one of the historic and greatest events in the life of the Israelites. The Bible is very clear about God's plan for them (the Israelites) and the mixed multitudes. God will give us good burdens and God glorifying burdens, but Satan will do the opposite. Satan will give us burdens to carry. You just name it. It could be physical burdens, emotional burdens and to some could be spiritual burdens. We struggle with financial burdens in life. And the sad thing is that we become in bondage of our own burdens and sin. Peter encouraged us when he said; "Casting all your care upon him; for he careth for you." (I Peter 5:7) The good thing is… we don't have to be in bondage of anything and by anyone, but of the Lord Jesus Christ; because in Him we have freedom. When Eliezer, JR and Eliel Lyn were little, they used to sing this song: "Cares Chorus…"

"I cast all my cares upon You
I lay all of my burdens down at Your feet
And anytime that I don't know what to do
I will cast all my cares upon You." Artist: Gospel Album:
Unknown

As you follow the Lord, you can cither be a burden bearer or a burden. You can either make things happen or you will just watch things happen. You will stand as Moses of these present times or be a Pharaoh or one of the Israelites of this present time. But one thing for sure, we know that God has all the reasons why He gave us burdens. We may have burdens but we know that God loves us so much. That is our assurance and comfort as we carry our burdens. You can either create your own burdens or you could become a victim of someone else's burden or wrong doings. "17- The righteous cry and the LORD heareth and delivereth them out of all their troubles. 18- The LORD is nigh unto them that are of a broken heart; and saveth such as be of a contrite spirit. 19- Many are the afflictions of the righteous: but the LORD delivereth him out of them all." (Psalm 55: 22; 34:17- 19)

THURSDAY

THE REASON FOR THEIR AFFLICTIONS AND SORROWS...

(Exodus 3:7- 8) "7- And the LORD said, I have surely seen the affliction of my people which are in Egypt, and have heard their cry by reason of their taskmasters; for I know their sorrows; 8- And I am come down to deliver them out of the hand of the Egyptians, and to bring them up out of that land unto a good land and a large, unto a land flowing with milk and honey; unto the place of the Canaanites, and the Hittites, and the Amorites, and the Perizzites, and the Hivites, and the Jebusites."

The 3 Sources of Our Burdens:

Burdens from the Lord... Jesus said; "28- Come unto me, all ye that labour and are heavy laden, and I will give you rest. 29- Take my yoke upon you, and learn of me; for I am meek and lowly in heart: and ye shall find rest unto your souls. 30- For my yoke is easy, and my burden is light." (Matthew 11:28-30) Apostle Paul wrote; "4- For we that are in this tabernacle do groan, being burdened: not for that we would be unclothed, but clothed upon, that mortality might be swallowed up of life." (II Corinthians 5:4)

Burdens from Satan... (The devil will send afflictions) "And the LORD said, I have surely seen the affliction of my people which are in Egypt, and have heard their cry by reason of their taskmasters; for I know their sorrows;" (Exodus 3:7) Take note of the words "affliction, taskmasters and sorrows" Affliction brings sorrows and the reason for affliction and sorrows were because of our taskmasters in our life. If you continue to submit yourself to your own taskmasters, you will live in afflictions and sorrow.

Burdens from fellow men... What is a task masters? Who are your taskmasters? You have to make a choice and don't be like the Israelites who lived under the power of their taskmasters for a long time. You may be wondering why you are still living a life that's not exactly where you wanted it to be and what you wanted to be. And you're not where God really wants you to be. It's because you are living under the hand of your taskmasters. You know that you're hook into it already, but you just don't know how to get out of it. Some people knew that they are addicted to something already, but they're just fine or ok with it. They won't even bother anymore. Getting used to it could be so dangerous to both Christians and the whole world. Once you keep on doing it, you will get used to it. You want to get out of the hands of your taskmasters, but you don't know how and which step to take. It's so easy: Jesus said: "Come unto me..." "Take my yoke..." and "Learn of me..." "28- Come unto me, all ye that labour and are heavy laden, and I will give you rest. 29- Take my yoke upon you, and learn of me; for I am meek and lowly in heart: and ye shall find rest unto your souls. 30- For my yoke is easy, and my burden is light." (Matthew 11:28- 30) *God has given us the grace and He is the One leading us.* "7- But unto every one of us is given grace according to the measure of the gift of Christ. 8- Wherefore he saith, When he ascended up on high, he led captivity captive, and gave gifts unto men." (Ephesians 4:7- 8)

FRIDAY
GOD'S COMMANDS FOR WORSHIP TO THE NEW TESTAMENT BELIEVERS.

(Exodus 20: 10 –11) "10- But the seventh day is the Sabbath of the LORD thy God; in it thou shalt not do any work, thou, nor thy son, nor thy daughter, thy manservant, nor thy maidservant, nor thy cattle, nor thy stranger that is within thy gates; 11- For in six days the LORD made heaven and earth, the sea, and all that in them is, and rested the seventh day; wherefore, the LORD blessed the Sabbath day, and hallowed it."

Meaning of Worship- Worship according to William Temple; "Is to quicken the conscious God, to feed the mind with the truth of God, to open up the heart to the love of God, to devote that will to the purpose of God." The word "Sabbath" and "Seventh" does not come from the same original word. The Hebrew for "Sabbath" is "Shabbath" meaning "Intermission" or "Cease"… from work.

"Shabbath" It means to "Repose", or to "Desist" from exertion or to "Rest" and such rest does not have to be on the seventh day. The LORD blessed the Sabbath day… As believers, we therefore must join Him so we can be blessed and we can experience His blessings and be a channel of His blessings. You will go where God's blessing is. God's spiritual blessing is in His church where Christians worship the Lord of the Sabbath. As children of God, we must therefore join God on His Sabbath. Do you value worship and your service for Him?

Worship is a Necessity, Importance or an Expression of our Love for God? It is very obvious that worship in the Bible is not just a religious ritual and practiced, but a family gathering in the presence of God. The Bible mentioned the whole members of the family which includes the servants, extended families and the animals. Wow! It reminds me of the missionary who visited our church. He shared to us that his church started in a pig pen. He said that the chapel that they used to use for worship was actually next to the pig pen until they turned the whole place into a place of worship. God's commands for worship to the Old Testament believers is recorded in (Exodus 31:12- 18)

Worship Must Not be Neglected by Anyone Especially the Believers. The Father said; "10 But the seventh day is the sabbath of the LORD thy God: in it thou shalt not do any work, thou, nor thy son, nor thy daughter, thy manservant, nor thy maidservant, nor thy cattle, nor thy stranger that is within thy gates:" (Exodus 20:10) Notice what the writer of the book of Hebrews said; "Not forsaking the assembling of ourselves together, as the manner of some is; but exhorting one another: and so much the more, as ye see the day approaching." (Hebrews 10:25)

Worship Will Never Cease Because in Heaven We Will Worship Day and Night. Apostle John in his vision wrote; "8- them six wings about him; and they were full of eyes within: and they rest not day and night, saying, Holy, holy, holy, Lord God Almighty, which was, and is, and is to come. 9- And when those beasts give glory and honour and thanks to him that sat on the throne, who liveth forever and ever," (Revelation 4:8- 9)

SATURDAY
DON'T PLAY AROUND ON SABBATH DAYS

(Numbers 15:32- 36) "32- And while the children of Israel were in the wilderness, they found a man that gathered sticks upon the sabbath day. 33- And they that found him gathering sticks brought him unto Moses and Aaron, and unto all the congregation. 34- And they put him in ward, because it was not declared what should be done to him. 35- And the LORD said unto Moses, The man shall surely be put to death: all the congregation shall stone him with stones without the camp. 36- And all the congregation brought him without the camp, and stoned him with stones, and he died; as the Lord commanded Moses."

In verse 32- it speaks of what would happen if the people will work on Sabbath day. Notice how the people were cooperating and how they all stood together for the truth. This is one of the verses in the Bible that mentioned of how the supposedly *minority* stood up in unity as *majority*. If compared to this present generation… this man belongs to the majority and he was accused of the minority for picking up sticks on Sabbath day. If this happens on winter time, he might have been out to pick up some sticks so he can set fire in his tent, so he and his family could get some heat. We may assume that he was cooking something in the kitchen and he runs out of sticks to finish up what he was cooking. And he has to go out and gather sticks. We don't know what exactly made this man do what he got to do. If you would analyze and study his physical situations, it was really of necessity on his part. I believe it was not something for pleasures, but could be for his family. I understand that sometimes you have work on Sundays, but try to always find some time to worship God. When we express our love for God, we worship Him. If we say we love God, then we must express that love by our worship to Him in any forms. You don't play around with God on Sabbath days.

I wonder why most of the best games, the championships and other special events happened on Sundays. The devil wanted to use the Lord's Day for his (the devil's) day and own purpose. But we know that he can mimic God's given activities and other things which belong to God and His people, but he can't be God. If you love God, you will not be ashamed of Him. You want to express your love to God in as many ways as possible. We obey our parents and we obey authorities like our employer or superior for various reasons. But it's too hard for us to obey God's Word. And sometimes we obey out of fear, because we are afraid of punishment or we're afraid of negative consequences. I read a material about worship and the author was talking about worshipping God in many forms and ways. Also, he said that we can worship God in our words, actions and all that we do. Indeed, in all that we do; we can bring honor, glory and praise to His holy name. Do it now for Jesus' sake and glory. Serve and worship God the Father! The Bible says; "...yet turn not aside from following the LORD, but serve the LORD with all your heart;" (Joshua 24:14) "Now therefore fear the LORD, and serve him in sincerity and in truth: and put away the gods which your fathers served on the other side of the flood, and in Egypt; and serve ye the LORD. (I Samuel 12:20) The books of (Exodus 23:25 and Deuteronomy 10:12) recorded the benefits of worship and in serving the Lord. Notice what John said; "This is love for God: to obey his commands, And his commands are not burdensome," (I John 5: 3)

SUNDAY
GOD'S COMMANDS FOR WORSHIP...

(Hebrews 10:25) "25- Not forsaking the assembling of ourselves together, as the manner of some is; but exhorting one another: and so much the more, as ye see the day approaching."

We have read of the example of the believers after the resurrection and pentecost. Worship is being practiced up to this present times (Acts 2: 40- 47). A marquee in Philippine International Christian Church of Trenton, Michigan says; *"One week without church makes one weak."* You may not know how much encouragement you gave your pastor when you showed up on Sundays for worship. Few years ago, the world watched the Philippine February Revolution live on Television. It was when millions of Filipinos gathered at EDSA (Epifanio De los Santos Avenue) against the then Philippine president Ferdinand E. Marcos. It was scary during those times as the tanks and armor carrier rolling down the major roads. And there were millions of people blocking the major roads. But one thing I've noticed during those times; churches were open 7 days a week and people came to their respective churches and religious organizations to worship. It also happens during the Aquino administration when they had a coup. We were so scared; because the military base and the soldiers who wanted to take the government from Mrs. Aquino were in a hotel few kilometers away from our church and in our home in Makati city. But we have worship on Sundays and special prayer meetings. If you remember days after the 9/11; people were so religious and millions of Americans started coming back to their churches and started to come to church on Sundays for worship. What's the message for us? That people would only come to church when they have problems? That people would only need God when they're in trouble? That we only seek God when our country is going through difficult times, in a civil war or in a war.? That church would not mean anything to some until life is not going the way they wanted it to be? One of the mistake and failure of many Christians is to pray. Mistake because many people and countries in the world pray, but in a wrong god. People pray in the name of the saints or in a wrong object or objects.

Remember the story of Daniel during the time of Nebuchadnezzar in (Daniel 3). Nebuchadnezzar made a declaration or a law where people were commanded to worship the image that he made. The prophet Daniel and the three young Hebrews refused to worship the god of Nebuchadnezzar. God will spare a nation, a home or an individual if we learn to pray. Remember during the time of Abraham when God talked to Abraham about God destroying Sodom and Gomorrah because of their pride and immorality (Genesis 18:20-33). And it's very unfortunate that we are going through the same problems in such a time as this. It's also unfortunate that some Christians, they worship the *worship*. Some believers have the philosophy of... "If your worship is not the same as mine, then I don't belong to your church or to this church." "If your music and the Bible translation your pastor is using is not the same as mine, then I'm not coming to your church. The focused is not in God and in worshipping Him in Spirit and in truth, but in personal preferences. (John 4:20- 24) It happened during the times of Jesus and it's still happening today! "46- And they, continuing daily with one accord in the temple, and breaking bread from house to house, did eat their meat with gladness and singleness of heart. 47- Praising God, and having favour with all the people, And the Lord added to the church daily such as should be saved." (Acts 2:46- 47)

MONDAY

GOD DESERVES OUR WORSHIP

(Psalm 99:1-3) "1- The LORD reigneth; let the people tremble: he sitteth between the cherubims; let the earth be moved. 2- The LORD is great in Zion; and he is high above all the people. 3- Let them praise thy great and terrible name; for it is holy."

God should be the foundation of all religions and beliefs, but we formed our own religion, our own gods and belief. Christianity is laid in the truth and that the Lord our God is the King of kings. He is the only Savior of the world and we believe in the holy trinity. God governs the world by his providence and sovereign will. He governs the church by his grace, and both by his Son. We must believe not only that the Lord lives, but that the Lord reigns. "The LORD reigneth and blessed be the Rock of my salvation" said the Psalmists. God is the one who ruleth the universe and if He is the ruler, then He deserves and is worthy of our worship. If you picture in your mind the greatness of God in verse 1, it indicates that we are unworthy of Him. "The LORD reigneth; let the people tremble: he sitteth between the cherubims; let the earth be moved." (Psalms 99:1) I- "The LORD who reigns…" And He reigns above all powers and kingdoms. II- And because He reigns…It makes sense when the writer said: "let the people trembles." III- "He sitteth between the Cherubims…" Because God is above all creations… so, "let the earth be moved." The next time you show up at church; put this in mind of who you are worshipping before you, as you approach the sanctuary of God. Worship God with this verse in mind and in your heart. *Worship and Exalt God.* (Psalm 99: 5; 8-9) The words *"Exalt", "Worship", "Call or Called" and "Holy"* was mentioned in out text at least twice or more. "Answeredst and forgavest…" were mentioned in verse 8. Our responsibilities and duties are to exalt God, to also worship Him as God's children and to call upon Him. He is a holy God and we are sinful and wicked. If Moses, Aaron and Samuel prayed to God and worship Him in His holiness, it seems just right for us who are unworthy before His presence to do the same. First and foremost; we're not as spiritual, pious and as close to God as His prophets. We are also a needy people. When we draw nigh to God to worship Him with all our hearts and our minds, we must remember to fill our thoughts of Him who is worthy of our praise. He must be exalted in our body, soul and spirit. The more we humble ourselves and the more we prostrate before God, the more we exalt Jesus as the King of kings and the Lord of lords. We must worship in His footstool and mercy-seat. No one else deserves the honor, glory and praise but the Jesus who died for my place. No one else deserves my love and worship, but God who is in the throne of grace. No one else deserves my service, but the Son of God who took the form of a servant and was made of no reputation. Paul wrote; "But made himself of no reputation, and took upon him the form of a servant, and was made in the likeness of men:"

Isaiah wrote; "2- Above it stood the seraphims: each one had six wings; with twain he covered his face, and with twain he covered his feet, and with twain he did fly. 3- And one cried unto another, and said, Holy, holy, holy, is the LORD of hosts: the whole earth is full of his glory." (Isaiah 6:2- 3)

TUESDAY
"JOY COMES IN THE MORNING"

(Psalms 30:5) "For his anger endureth but a moment; in his favour is life: weeping may endure for a night, but joy cometh in the morning."

"Joy comes in the morning..." For me it means "after the darkness or after the dark night". After the intense pain; then Joy comes in the morning... After the long wait in the dark side of the night (dark side of life because of trials)- then we have the morning light or sun rise, the new day and new beginning. "I am weary of my crying: my throat is dried: mine eyes fail while I wait for my God." (Psalms 69:3) God is always there to give us *song in the night.* (Psalms 77:2-6) Remember that at the back of the clouds, the sun is always shinning. God is in control and He is always in control no matter what your situations in life right now. Praise God because "Joy comes in the morning as you learn to worship, serve and give for His name's sake.

- Worship- "Not forsaking the assembling of ourselves together, as the manner of some is; but exhorting one another: and so much the more, as ye see the day approaching." (Hebrews 10:25)

- Serve- "And Samuel spake unto all the house of Israel, saying, If ye do return unto the LORD with all your hearts, then put away the strange gods and Ashtaroth from among you, and prepare your hearts unto the LORD, and serve him only: and he will deliver you out of the hand of the Philistines." (I Samuel 7:3)

- Give- "It's not what's in your pocket or bank account and what you have at home that will make you thankful, but what's in your heart." You have Jesus the Savior of the world and He owns everything. The prince of preacher said; "If you only serve for the applause of men, you sacrifice the approval of God. As Christ's followers, we should not be surprised if the service we render to others in Jesus' name is unappreciated or even spurned." Keep serving the Lord in spite of... and in the midst of... whether you have blessings or trials. *Give!* (II Corinthians 8:1) 1- you have the heart for true *worship*, you will surely learn to *serve* and *give*." When Jesus showed Himself to the disciples in different occasions on that resurrection day; it was a blessed day and a day of joy and blessings. They worship Him and give themselves to God first. God desires your heart more than anything else... He wants your heart of worship. Verses 19 to 20, it says; "19- Speaking to yourselves in psalms and hymns and spiritual songs, singing and making melody in your heart to the Lord; 20- Giving thanks always for all things unto God and the Father in the name of our Lord Jesus Christ;" Be joyful, sing and worship the Lord our God. God's grace enables us to face the music... even when we don't like the tunes. It is possible to have tears in our eyes, while there is song in our heart. That's exactly what David as God's servant went through and said. Songs and singing is not only for good times but also for bad times. Music is not only for time of blessings, but in times of pain and sorrow. People have different reasons for singing. You can sing for money, for fame, to please people and for your own pleasure, but Christians sings to express our gratefulness to God and to bring honor to His holy name. We sing as an expression of our love and worship to Him. It's easy to do that when you're at church or in a mountain top experience, but it would be a different story if you're in a tough and rough road. It would be a different story if you're in a situations like Job or Joseph of the Old Testament and the Apostle Paul when he was in prison. The Bible encourages us to sing and make melody in our heart for God's glory, to be joyful and to rejoice. You need to *Worship Him* and sing for Him...? (Colossians 3:16- 17)

WEDNESDAY
BE *GOD'S MAN* IN YOUR WORLD
(Galatians 2:20)

"I am crucified with Christ: nevertheless I live; yet not I, but Christ liveth in me: and the life which I now live in the flesh I live by the faith of the Son of God, who loved me, and gave himself for me."

I believe that Paul lived a life that truly honors the Lord Jesus Christ. Paul was a man to be admired: 1- Because of his *gratefulness* (I Thessalonians 5:18). 2- Because of his *prayerfulness* (I Thessalonians 5:17; Romans 1:9). 3- Because of his *joy* (Philippians 4:4). In spite of his uncomfortable and really bad situations, Apostle Paul has joy in his heart. If Paul would be given a chance to live again in this modern world; I'm very much sure, Paul would not be concern of building huge chapels or church buildings but saintly saints. He will not plant seed of corruption and destruction, but the seed of regeneration and a changed life. Indeed Paul was a man of God. Paul was a lawyer who became a preacher. Paul was a persecutor who became a propagator. He was a sinner who became a saint. Paul was the true disciple of the Lord Jesus Christ. Walter A. Henrichsen said; "The disciple is one who in every area of his life determines from the Bible what is right and lives it consistently. The disciple is one who is in constant touch with people in need."

How can you be the man of God in your world? It starts with being born again. It starts with: *Salvation.* You have to have Christ in you; He is *"the only way"* to heaven. But you have to follow these steps:

- Accept Christ in your heart as your Savior and Lord. "But as many as received him, to them gave he power to become the sons of God, even to them that believe on his name:" (John 1:12)

- Believe in Him that He alone can save you and forgive you of your sins. (I John 1:8-9)

- Confess your sins and confess Christ that He is God, Savior and Lord.

Surrender Your Life to God as a Living Sacrifice. When D. L. Moody heard a Layman preached about surrender, Mr. Moody surrendered his life to God that day and he said: "God has yet to see what God can do to a fully yielded, surrendered man." D. L. Moody said, "I will be that man". And the rest is history... You have to leave a legacy that your family and friends will treasure someday. They could always look back and say something good about you. Apostle Paul said, "I bear in my body the marks of the Lord Jesus Christ..." It will remind us of his love for the Lord and his faithfulness to God and the Lord's ministry. Be a man in your world... Paul said; "1- I beseech you therefore, brethren, by the mercies of God, that ye present your bodies a living sacrifice, holy, acceptable unto God, which is your reasonable service. 2- And be not conformed to this world: but be ye transformed by the renewing of your mind, that ye may prove what is that good, and acceptable, and perfect, will of God." (Romans 12:1-2)

THURSDAY

FREE GIFTS- GOOD DEAL AND A GREAT DEAL

(Ephesians 2:8- 10) "8- For by grace are ye saved through faith; and that not of yourselves: it is the gift of God: 9-Not of works, lest any man should boast.10- For we are his workmanship, created in Christ Jesus unto good works, which God hath before ordained that we should walk in them."

A good friend of mine one day said to me: "Ely, the best thing in life is free." It's true, especially when it comes to spiritual matters. We got something from the mail which offers us a free cruise to the Bahamas for 4 to 7 days. Sometimes a free air fare for 2 to Orlando, Florida or Hawaii. And many other offers like free computer or lap top. But we already know that you have to pay for it in some ways or there's always a catch. But not with God and what the holy Bible promises to those who comes to God for *FREE…*

First, we have the free gift of salvation from God and in the Lord Jesus Christ. We received eternal life as a free gift. "For the wages of sin is death; but the gift of God is eternal life through Jesus Christ our Lord." (Romans 6: 23) We will spend eternity in heaven with Jesus. (John 14:1- 6) Notice what Apostle Paul said in (Titus 3: 4- 5) "4- But after that the kindness and love of God our Saviour toward man appeared, 5- Not by works of righteousness which we have done, but according to his mercy he saved us, by the washing of regeneration, and renewing of the Holy Ghost;"

Secondly, we have God's gift of forgiveness for our sins and trespasses. (Ephesians 1:6- 7) "6-To the praise of the glory of his grace, wherein he hath made us accepted in the beloved. 7- In whom we have redemption through his blood, the forgiveness of sins, according to the riches of his grace;" (Ephesians 4:31- 32) The Lord by His grace opened the door of forgiveness to everyone including the chief among sinners like the Apostle Paul. God forgave Moses who killed an Egyptian. God forgave King David when he committed adultery with Bathsheba and killed Uriah to cover up his sins. (II Samuel 11: 1- 27) If God forgave them, He can forgive you too. Be it a weakness, a moral issue or it's just too big of a sin on your part, God's blood can cleanse you of any sin or sins. "The next day John seeth Jesus coming unto him, and saith, Behold the Lamb of God, which taketh away the sin of the world." (John 1:29) Trust the Lord for your salvation. You don't only accept Him as your Lord and Savior, but you will have to trust Him and believe in Jesus. We visited the Coca-Cola plant in Atlanta, Georgia. We checked on one of the rooms where you can see all kinds of coke from all over the world. One of the things that you'll be amazed with is the free taste of all kinds of cokes from different countries of the world. You can drink for free and it's as much as you want. God is giving as something more important and great than anything this world can offer. We have the free gift of salvation through the Lord Jesus Christ.

The Bible said; "30- And brought them out, and said, Sirs, what must I do to be saved? 31- And they said, Believe on the Lord Jesus Christ, and thou shalt be saved, and thy house." (Psalm 37:40; Psalm 49:6- 8) 6- "They that trust in their wealth, and boast themselves in the multitude of their riches; 7- None of them can by any means redeem his brother, nor give to God a ransom for him: 8- For the redemption of their soul is precious, and it ceaseth forever:)" (Acts 16:30- 31)

FRIDAY

SAMSON'S LOVE LIFE WAS NOT HEALTHY

(Judges 16: 17) "17- That he told her all his heart, and said unto her, There hath not come a razor upon mine head; for I have been a Nazarite unto God from my mother's womb: if I be shaven, then my strength will go from me, and I shall become weak, and be like any other man."

Samson was a Nazarite but Jesus was a Nazarene. There were only 3 people in the whole Bible that were called Nazarites: John, Samuel and Samson. What leads Samson to ask God his causeless death wish? What was the cause of Samson's miseries, grief and causeless life and prayers? What made him so mad and miserable? "32- But whoso committeth adultery with a woman lacketh understanding: he that doeth it destroyeth his own soul. 33- A wound and dishonour shall he get; and his reproach shall not be wiped away." (Proverbs 6:32- 33) Adultery, pride and choosing the wrong life partner were the primary reasons of his downfall. (Judges 14: 1- 4; 16: 4). Samson loved the wrong woman, the unbeliever and the wife of the uncircumcised Philistines. He married a woman with a wrong purpose. He married a woman according to his fleshly desires. Samson said to his father: "Get her for me; for she pleaseth me well…" Samson made a big mistake and committed sin when he went in with harlot. "Then went Samson to Gaza, and saw there an harlot, and went in unto her." And then he felt in love with another woman- this time it was with Delilah. ((Judges 16:1; 4) I've seen Christians and ministers who fell into sin of adultery. Their homes, their relationship with God and love ones were broken by such sin. The beauty of their lives, the joy and peace of their homes and their growing ministries and church were destroyed because of sin. And their healthy relationship as well as their hope and their dreams and future were all gone. Samson's love life was not healthy because he was not practicing a healthy life style in his private life as God's servant. Samson was idle. It means that he was not doing anything. He was just chatting with Delilah. I like Facebook and I like email and the internet. We enjoy some of the good things that we have about internet and chatting. I believe that they're a blessing to this present generation; but it could cause a lot of problems. Samson lost his moral value after wasting so much of his time by chatting with Delilah. He was idle, got tempted, he grabbed the temptation and he fell into sin. Does it sound familiar to many of your friends? If you're a victim of Satan's temptation to idleness and for not being a good steward of your time; try to ask the Lord to forgive you and make a big U-turn. Keep yourself busy for the Lord.

Samson also listened to the voice of the enemy. Satan can use anyone, even the closest person in your life including your family circle to lead you to a sinful life style. Satan can put words in the lips of your friends and love ones to destroy you and to cause you to fall in your faith and relationship with God. The Bible said; "5- And the lords of the Philistines came up unto her, and said unto her, Entice him, and see wherein his great strength lieth, and by what means we may prevail against him, that we may bind him to afflict him: and we will give thee every one of us eleven hundred pieces of silver. 6- And Delilah said to Samson, Tell me, I pray thee, wherein thy great strength lieth, and wherewith thou mightest be bound to afflict thee." (Judges 16:5- 6)

SATURDAY

HE LOST HIS STRENGTH... BECAUSE OF SIN

(Judges 16:19- 21) "19- And she made him sleep upon her knees; and she called for a man, and she caused him to shave off the seven locks of his head; and she began to afflict him, and his strength went from him. 20- And she said, The Philistines be upon thee, Samson. And he awoke out of his sleep, and said, I will go out as at other times before, and shake myself. And he wist not that the LORD was departed from him. 21- But the Philistines took him, and put out his eyes, and brought him down to Gaza, and bound him with fetters of brass; and he did grind in the prison house."

Millions of people all over the world are living a causeless life. They're living a life without purpose. Samson suffered in living without a cause. After Samson was deceived by his so called lover-Delilah, he lived a causeless life. I heard a pastor friend of mine preached about "Living Worst than Death" and he talked about those who have lived a purposeless and causeless life. They are the kind of people who lives their life miserably and death is the only answer for them. *Samson lost his strength* and he became a laughing stock to his enemies, the Philistines. The enemies made fun of him and the God we served because of his sin. Samson lost his physical strength as well as his spiritual strength. (Judges 16:19) "...and his strength went from him." Samson was the strongest man in the world, but he was very weak when it comes to women. I believe Samson knew what his weakness was, but Samson just took it for granted. He lost his strength which was really from the Lord and it was not because of sickness, but God took it from him. Samson messed it up. You can't play around with your weakness or weaknesses. In terms of food, my weaknesses are nuts and pizza and I'm not supposed to eat so much of those; but sometimes I just want to eat and eat. It's so hard to resist the temptation of eating foods that are against the will of your doctor and spouse; but the will of your flesh is stronger than anybody in this world. Coffee and tea are in my blood already, but moderation and control is the key. We are all into this in some ways, but we need to exercise discipline. My father and mother will not be here to control me and to keep me out of what is not a balanced diet, but I have to eat and drink healthy. In our spiritual life, we should do the same. Exercise our faith, discipline, control and moderation.

Your pastor and Sunday school teacher will not be there for you all the time, but you have to be disciplined, dedicated and be devoted to God and His Word. Samson failed to do them. (Judges 14:1-3) "I would rather live a life destitute of the world's goodness and wealth than to live a life destitute of the presence of God." You may look prosperous in the sight of man; but you cannot hide the anguish, the grief, the anxiety, the guilt and the hopelessness inside of you. I know of a friend who lost his wealth for the sake of God, while there are those who lost their homes, their strength in the Lord because of sin. There are churches that you cannot even feel God's presence as you step in the door up to the sanctuary. There's no joy, there's no power in the preaching of the Word of God. Samson lost his strength and his power from God because of sin. It did not happened in one day; it was a process that Samson was not even aware of. According to Matthew Henry commentary on Philippians 4: 6- "The word *to epieikes* signifies a good disposition towards other men; and this moderation is explained, Rom. 14. Some understand it of the patient bearing of afflictions, or the sober enjoyment of worldly good; and so it well agrees with the following verse. The reason is *the Lord is at hand.*" (The Bible Collection Suite) "Let your moderation be known unto all men. The Lord is at hand." (Philippians 4: 6)

SUNDAY

AS LONG AS OUR PRAYER IS UNTO THE LORD

(Psalm 69: 13) "But as for me, my prayer is unto thee, O LORD, in an acceptable time: O God, in the multitude of thy mercy hear me, in the truth of thy salvation."

How often, how long, how sincere, how earnest, how do you pray? Those are some of the questions people asked. Others are so conscious of their physical position when they pray or as they pray. God is more interested in our inside attitude than with our outside expressions in prayer. Hannah went up to the house of the Lord... and she wept. It was when Hannah was praying for a son. "7- And as he did so year by year, when she went up to the house of the LORD, so she provoked her; therefore she wept, and did not eat. 10- And she was in bitterness of soul, and prayed unto the LORD, and wept sore." (I Samuel 1:7; 10) "Surrender" means "hands up, down on your knees to God and you bow down your head in the spirit of humility." Apostle Paul has a different way of praying, he has different desires and requests to God *"9 - For God is my witness, whom I serve with my spirit in the gospel of his Son, that without ceasing I make mention of you always in my prayers; 10- Making request, if by any means now at length I might have a prosperous journey by the will of God to come unto you."* (Romans 1:9- 10) "Failure" means "a ladder to success, if you will not look down but look up." As for King Solomon, he has a different story. His desire and prayer requests were so different from other kings, prophets and servants of God including the rulers and soldiers of God. (II Chronicles 1:7- 12) Let me share this outline bout prayer and I hope this will be of help to you:

- God Wants Us to Call Unto Him. It means to pray. God said; "Call unto me..." (Jeremiah 33:3)

- God's Will is to Answer Our Prayers. God said; "Call unto me... and I will answer thee..."(Jeremiah 33:3)

- God Way of Working in Us is to Enrich Us with Blessings and Power. *Enrich means to make rich, To supply with an abundance with anything desirable".* (Ephesians 3:20; Philippians 4:19)

Hyman J. Appelman wrote; "Prayerlessness is a curse, but prayer is a cure for all ills. Prayer has determined the course of Christendom." (Appelman's Sermon Outlines and Illustrations, Zonderdervan Publishing House, Grand Rapids, Michigan).We need to pray and pray more and really pray hard at home and in our churches. The Lord Jesus Christ prayed to the Father when He was here on earth. Some of the verses in John chapter seventeen are the records of the Lord's Prayer. King David has a different story when it comes to prayer. David prayed for his enemies and he prayed constantly as well. "16- As for me, I will call upon God; and the LORD shall save me. 17- Evening, and morning, and at noon, will I pray, and cry aloud: and he shall hear my voice." (Psalms 55:16- 17)

MONDAY

HE LIVED IN SUFFERING

(Judges 16:19- 20) "19- And she made him sleep upon her knees; and she called for a man, and she caused him to shave off the seven locks of his head; and she began to afflict him, and his strength went from him. 20- And she said, The Philistines be upon thee, Samson. And he awoke out of his sleep, and said, I will go out as at other times before, and shake myself. And he wist not that the LORD was departed from him."

Samson suffered in living under the hands of his enemies and the enemies of God- the Philistines. Samson suffered in living a defeated life. The enemies made fun of him and used him for their own pleasures. And Satan can do the same to us Christians. "And it came to pass, when their hearts were merry, that they said, Call for Samson, that he may make us sport. And they called for Samson out of the prison house; and he made them sport: and they set him between the pillars." (Judges 16: 25) Samson also lived in blindness after the enemies took off his 2 eyes. The Philistines knew that if Samson would be blind, they can control him and they don't have to live in fear of Samson's getting back on them. If you would just think of how the devil operates and how they works in their vicious desire to destroy God's children and God's work has not changed. I wish everyone would see the big pictures on how the devil made billions of followers by blinding the spiritual eyes of the world. Samson lost control over his own life because he was blind. Billions of people all over the world lost control of their lives, of their family, of their business, of their spiritual life and you can think of millions of things that causes blindness in our lives. Money, power, position and possessions can cause spiritual blindness. What happened to Samson is happening to this present generation. Samson suffered and lived a defeated life because of blindness. In verse 21 is a bad picture of a man who was once the strongest, powerful, religious and a family man. Now check out what happened to him as he suffered in the hands of the enemies: They: "took him", "put out his eyes", "and brought him down…", "bound him" and "…he grind in the prison house." The Bible said; "But the Philistines took him, and put out his eyes, and brought him down to Gaza, and bound him with fetters of brass; and he did grind in the prison house." (Judges 16: 21)We need to have a constant self- examination of our heart and mind. It's our personal check and balances. (I Peter 3:13- 18)

Matthew Henry wrote; "The extremity of the church and people of God is Christ's opportunity to visit them and appear for them: but he came not till *the fourth watch,* toward three o'clock in the morning, for then the fourth watch began. It was *in the morning-watch* that the Lord appeared for Israel in the Red sea (Ex. 14:24)" (The Bible Collection, Matthew Henry)

This could be the same message that Peter will share to Samson; "12- Beloved, think it not strange concerning the fiery trial which is to try you, as though some strange thing happened unto you: 13- But rejoice, inasmuch as ye are partakers of Christ's sufferings; that, when his glory shall be revealed, ye may be glad also with exceeding joy. 14- If ye be reproached for the name of Christ, happy are ye; for the spirit of glory and of God resteth upon you: on their part he is evil spoken of, but on your part he is glorified. 15- But let none of you suffer as a murderer, or as a thief, or as an evildoer, or as a busybody in other men's matters. 16- Yet if any man suffer as a Christian, let him not be ashamed; but let him glorify God on this behalf." (I Peter 4:12- 16)

TUESDAY

HE LOST IT ALL!

(Judges 16:25) "And it came to pass, when their hearts were merry, that they said, Call for Samson, that he may make us sport. And they called for Samson out of the prison house; and he made them sport: and they set him between the pillars."

Have you ever had that experience? You can't feel the presence of God in your life. Samson dishonor God by not pleasing the Lord who gave him the strength. Samson was brought down to his lowest point. He was humbled by the Lord because of his sin. I believe that Samson repented of the sins he committed and as a result in verse 22; it appears like Samson was reconciled to God and in the process of time, his *Nazariteship* if there is such a word or his vow as a Nazarite was beginning to return as his hair began to grow. "Howbeit the hair of his head began to grow again after he was shaven." Those were the days when Samson began to feel the presence of God again. In verse "30- And Samson said, Let me die with the Philistines. And he bowed himself with all his might; and the house fell upon the lords, and upon all the people that were therein. So the dead which he slew at his death were more than they which he slew in his life." So, when Samson prayed to God for strength, God granted his prayer and got his strength back. Samson destroyed the whole house full of people.

If you will have your last words on your death bed or if you would want to leave a will or have your last prayer; I'm very much sure it will not be like this, in verse "28- And Samson called unto the LORD, and said, O Lord GOD, remember me, I pray thee, and strengthen me, I pray thee, only this once, O God, that I may be at once avenged of the Philistines for my two eyes." Who would want to be like Samson? He was a man who would rather die than live in blindness, used for fun and let the enemies make a sport out of him. He became the enemies' instrument for their own pleasures and an instrument to dishonor God and give honor to their god Dagon. Samson was a loser, but he did not want to die a loser so he prayed for God's help and blessings. At least in his last breathed, he died praying and standing against the enemies of God. We witnessed similar stories like this at home, in hospice and in the hospital where people died with their last words… It's so sad when we see people died a miserable death or died in misery. You may know of someone who died or about to die a loser because of sins. It was different with Elijah when he desired death. The Bible said; "But he himself went a day's journey into the wilderness, and came and sat down under a juniper tree: and he requested for himself that he might die; and said, It is enough; now, O LORD, take away my life; for I am not better than my fathers." (I Kings 19:4) Jonah has a different story and reasons why he desired death…"Therefore now, O LORD, take, I beseech thee, my life from me; for it is better for me to die than to live." (Jonah 4:3) Take the advice of Apostle Paul: "57- But thanks be to God, which giveth us the victory through our Lord Jesus Christ. 58- "Therefore, my beloved brethren, be ye steadfast, unmoveable, always abounding in the work of the Lord, forasmuch as ye know that your labour is not in vain in the Lord." (I Corinthians 15: 57- 58)

WEDNESDAY
WICKEDNESS OVERTHROWETH THE SINNER

(Proverbs 13:6, 9) "6- Righteousness keepeth him that is upright in the way: but wickedness overthroweth the sinner. 9- The light of the righteous rejoiceth: but the lamp of the wicked shall be put out."

The verses are a comparison between evil and good. It was Solomon's personal experienced on what the evil and the good, sin and righteousness will do to us. Solomon experienced them as God's servant. The pain and the consequences of sin and the joy of righteousness and its God given reward for those who practiced them. King Solomon, the man who is full of wisdom warned us:

- (Proverbs 4: 14) *"Enter not into the path of the wicked..."* It's a warning for us not to enter into the gates of sin and practicing sinners. *ENTER NOT-* the ticket to enter in into their path is free, but you have to pay for the consequences. In (Proverbs 4:15) it says, "Avoid it, pass not by it, turn from it, and pass away."

- *"Avoid it..."* The writer knows that going to the place of sinners is dangerous. And the way to overcome is to avoid the temptation of entering into it. Not even to pass by it. In (Proverbs 4: 17) it says, "For they eat the bread of wickedness, and drink the wine of violence." It is so obvious that wickedness is their life. They eat and drink in wickedness and in darkness. In (Proverbs 4: 19) "The way of the wicked is as darkness: they know not at what they stumble." Praise God (Proverbs 4:18) "But the path of the just is as the shining light, that shineth more and more unto the perfect day." As Christians, we are the light of the world and the Bible says that our "...path is as the shining light." We all went through temptations and we will go through to a lot more while we are here on earth. It means that temptation is part of the cycle of the Christian life.

It's very unfortunate that people are working against the will of God and are entering in into the arena of the devil and many of them are not aware of their spiritual condition. The only way out to those who gets in into the devil's arena is repentance unto the Lord. "Avoid" and "Enter not" are the words that we, as believers of the Lord Jesus Christ should be aware of.

In (I Corinthians 10:9– 13) Paul warned us of not tempting the Lord Jesus Christ. So temptation could be from us to God. It means that we should not put God to the test, lest we suffer the consequences of our sins as the Israelites did when they cling upon their lusts. (Exodus chapter 32) For Christians, the Lord promised us of deliverance, but you have to live a godly life. He said, "The Lord knoweth how to deliver the godly out of temptations…" We need to be strong in the faith because Satan, our enemy is not taking a "time out" in his effort to deceive and destroy both Christians and his very own. Sometimes Satan would start from a cookie in a cookie jar. He starts small to destroy big people, huge ministries and large amount of damages both in physical, financial, moral, emotional and spiritual life of a man or a woman. We know that prayer and the Word of God are our weapons against the wiles of the devil. We must use it to resist the enemy. "The Lord knoweth how to deliver the godly out of temptations, and to reserve the unjust unto the day of judgment to be punished:" (II Peter 2:9)

THURSDAY

LET THEM KNOW THAT "JESUS IS COMING SOON"

(Luke 8:1) "And it came to pass afterward, that he went throughout every city and village, preaching and showing the glad tidings of the kingdom of God: and the twelve were with him,"

We have to get busy and get the job done. Do the work of an evangelist. Paul did not say that you must be an evangelist, but to *do the work of an evangelist*. What's the work of an evangelist? It is to tell others about Jesus and the gospel of the kingdom of God. They go from place to place, from town to town, from city to city and so on… It means they go everywhere and anywhere. And they keep themselves busy for the work of the Lord. Whether people will accept Him or not or whether Christians will obey His commands to go or not… "Jesus is coming soon… and He will come again. *Praise God!* This kind of message… if I would just think about it, I felt like I wanted to shout 'Hallelujah' even in public. Christ is coming for us again. He fulfilled everything that was said regarding His coming without failure. The Apostles looked forward to His coming during their time here on earth. And we are rest assured of Christ's coming. These and many more are the assurance that Jesus is coming and we are to watch and pray and admonished one another. We must receive, believe, and obey God's Word.

James T. Dyet said: "Someone has observed that old age is God's way of telling us that warranty is running out." I know some of us can't just wait for Christ's coming. The whole wide world don't get any better, it's just getting worst and worst. Our inspiration in watching should be the Word of God, the Holy Spirit, and the truth. Rapture may come at any time. The world must know the way of God. We are not talking about the way to God, but God's way. May we have the same question Paul asked the Lord during his encounter with Jesus: "Lord, what do you want me to do?" But the issue could be; "how do you want me to do it?" "How does God want me to do it?" To know God's way, it means for us to abstain from fornication. (I Thessalonians 4:3) According to Webster dictionary, "Fornication" means "incontinence of unmarried persons." This is a reference to sexual sins in general. To know God's way it means for us not to defraud our brother in any matter. Apostle Paul said; "That no man go beyond and defraud his brother in any matter: because that the Lord is the avenger of all such, as we also forwarned you and testified." (I Thessalonians 4:6) To know God's way it means for us to *Love* the brethren. (I Thessalonians 4:9) This part of the Scripture should serve as an encouragement to every Christian and a warning to non- believers. This is our blessed hope and I always look forward to it. That blessed day when we shall see Him face to face- our Lord and Savior Jesus Christ without going through death. "15- For this we say unto you by the word of the Lord, that we which are alive and remain unto the coming of the Lord shall not prevent them which are asleep. 16- For the Lord himself shall descend from heaven with a shout, with the voice of the archangel, and with the trump of God: and the dead in Christ shall rise first: 17- Then we which are alive and remain shall be caught up together with them in the clouds, to meet the Lord in the air: and so shall we ever be with the Lord. 18- Wherefore comfort one another with these words." (I Thessalonians 4:15- 18)

FRIDAY
SOLOMON'S WISDOM AND COUNSELS

(Proverbs 5:1- 2) "1- My son, attend unto my wisdom, and bow thine ear to my understanding: 2- That thou mayest regard discretion, and that thy lips may keep knowledge."

As you grow, be it in spiritual, in physical, in business or in sports; you learn from reading, getting some advice or from your personal experience. Yes, we will for sure get an advice from a friend or love ones. You will get good counsel or advice, bad advice and sometimes unsolicited advice. In (Proverbs 6:6) "Go to the ant, thou sluggard; consider her ways, and be wise:" There must be something in the ants that human being should learn. When we were in Belize, we were told by a tourists guide in the jungle about ants and how they work hard in unity. And he actually showed us the big ants and their pattern. In (Proverbs 5:1- 2) Solomon was addressing himself to his son in verse 1- he said "My son..." Many of us are physically young, spiritually young and some are young in experience in life in general. Solomon said, "...attend unto my wisdom" "bow thine ear to my understanding." Notice the 4 important words: *"attend"* *"wisdom"* *"bow"* and *"understanding"*.

"Aim" means "acting wisely and with sobriety towards your goals, by the inspiration of the Holy Spirit of God, as you reach out for the Master's plan."

"Act" means "acting on a matter wisely and with a purpose of honoring God, and be committed to do it whatever it takes, and be thankful to God for the results." Now that is wisdom, it's when you act wisely and with sobriety. Peter said, *"Be sober because the devil is like a roaring lion..."* I am so glad to be able to share God's wisdom to my children by letting them know the truth of the Word of God. The Bible is the only source of wisdom that we have, because we may read (although not even a dot) of the mind of God as we read the Word of God. The Bible is the revelation of God's heart and mind as well as His revelation of what will happen in the future. You do not separate wisdom and understanding because as you learn from the Lord, you learn from this world too. "He that hath an ear, let him hear what the Spirit saith unto the churches." (Revelation 2:29) Open your ears and your heart to Christ who died on the cross for your sins. Be ready to hear what the Spirit is saying to you and put them into practice. Exercise and apply Solomon's wisdom and understanding in your daily life. Read the book of Proverbs every day at least a chapter a day. Another advice from the wisest man that ever lived is in (Proverbs 5:2) "That thou mayest regard discretion …" Someone made a comment about this verse, he said: "So you may act wisely and not blindly." Even king Solomon who is a king with a kingdom, needs the wisdom of the King of kings.

(Proverbs 1: 1- 7; II Timothy 3: 10- 13) Here are some of the benefits of living a godly life as promised to us in the Word of God; "The Lord knoweth how to deliver the godly out of temptations, and to reserve the unjust unto the day of judgment to be punished:" (II Peter 2: 9)

SATURDAY

"CHASTISEMENT"- NOT A PLEASANT WORD

(Hebrews 12:8) "But if ye be without chastisement, whereof all are partakers, then are ye bastards, and not sons."

Who would want to be chastised anyways? The word many Christians wanted to avoid and keep their ears closed. Chastisement is essential in our Christian life because it keeps us intimate in our relationship with God. Chastisement indeed is not a pleasant word, but a word to which it opens the doors of opportunity and blessings to Christians. It's a word which many Christians may not get the whole pictures of what lies ahead. It's a word and a way in which God used to instruct, to test, to give importance, to show, to indicate and give us the assurance that God loves us so much. He gave us the chastisement to get our attention for Him. Chastisement is a blessing from the Lord, because it gives us a good identification of the legitimacy of our relationship with God the Father. It means we are God's children if we have chastisement according to the writer of Hebrews; "7- If ye endure chastening, God dealeth with you as with sons; for what son is he whom the father chasteneth not? 8- But if ye be without chastisement, whereof all are partakers, then are ye bastards, and not sons." (Hebrews 12:7- 8) In my own understanding and belief as what the Bible said; chastisement is one of *God's signature in our birth certificate as a born again Christians.* The Lord has given us also a *good sign* that we are legitimate. God has given us also the *great support* that no one could give, which is the loving correction of God. I'm talking about spiritual dealings. Let us try to live up to that name- "Christian". We are His name bearer and we were called by that name. We bear His holy name to this sinful world. As I mentioned; we are His children and because we are His children, then it is in His power and prerogative to discipline us if we are not living accordingly. The Lord rebuked us, reminded us, and caused us to remember that which is pleasing to Him. "Furthermore we have had fathers of our flesh which corrected us, and we gave them reverence: shall we not much rather be in subjection unto the Father of spirits, and live?" (Hebrews 12:9) Charles Haddon Spurgeon the prince of preachers once said; "It is not my remembering God, it is God's remembering me that is the ground for my safety." He continued; "Even the remembrance of the covenant is not left to our memories. We might forget, but our Lord cannot forget the saints whom He has inscribed on the palms of His hands." (Isaiah 49:16) Peter knew what it meant to be in the arena of trials and sufferings. He wrote; "14- But and if ye suffer for righteousness' sake, happy are ye: and be not afraid of their terror, neither be troubled; 15- But sanctify the Lord God in your hearts: and be ready always to give an answer to every man that asketh you a reason of the hope that is in you with meekness and fear: 16- Having a good conscience; that, whereas they speak evil of you, as of evildoers, they may be ashamed that falsely accuse your good conversation in Christ. 17- For it is better, if the will of God be so, that ye suffer for well doing, than for evil doing. 18- For Christ also hath once suffered for sins, the just for the unjust, that he might bring us to God, being put to death in the flesh, but quickened by the Spirit:" (I Peter 3:14- 18)

SUNDAY
"AFTER THE BIG CHRISTMAS CELEBRATION... WHAT?"

(John 14: 17) "Even the Spirit of truth; whom the world cannot receive, because it seeth him not, neither knoweth him: but ye know him; for he dwelleth with you, and shall be in you."

I was on the Internet just a few minutes before I typed in the topic for Mi Daily Devotion and I left for a few seconds and when I came back on line... guess what's on the top of Yahoo Search... "After Christmas..." And I was just thinking about this subject while I was watching TV with my youngest son EJ that night. Elmer John said; "It would be another 365 days before Christmas." And after a while EJ said; "Now that Christmas is almost over..." EJ was already looking forward of celebrating next year's Christmas.

We have after Christmas sale, after Christmas best deals, after Christmas sales tips and the after Christmas clean ups. After Christmas check and balance of credit cards debt and the check and balance of our bank account. Checking on how much you've gain or lose because of so much food and stress. But remember to keep the Spirit of Christmas in our hearts. The Christmas celebration is on December 25, but the Spirit of Christmas must be 24/7, 365 or 366 days a year. Don't leave the spirit of Christmas on the table, in your unwrapped gifts or in your Christmas tree. Keep it in your hearts as you keep the Lord's commandment. We can keep the spirit of Christmas with God's love and our devotion to Him and Him alone. Let His Spirit, God's Spirit dwell in you. The Baby in a manger more than 2,000 years ago changed my life. He changed my heart, He changed my perspective, He changed my way of thinking, He changed my direction and I can go on and on...That little baby in the manger did not remain a baby and did not remain in a manger. He grew up in an "unpleasant place" called Nazareth. He was born in a very small city of Bethlehem which means the "house of bread." He grew up as a very wise boy, a little boy who is full of wisdom and knowledge that even the doctors and lawyers asked questions on Him. (Luke 2:39- 40) If you will just look at this little boy from the manger to Nazareth; imagine how He would become a good teacher, a healer, a writer and the greatest philanthropist in the world since the time of Adam and Eve up to the present; it's beyond our imagination. The little baby in that little manger with the sheep and other animals is the Savior of the world. He is the Messiah and the King of kings. He is the one who shaped up my life and He can do the same to you. He is the one who showed me the way from darkness to glory. He is the one who gave us joy, peace and satisfaction that this old world could never do. He is the CHRIST of Christmas, the only reason for the season and the center of the celebration. He is the reason why we have the steadfast love of the Lord. He is the Alpha and Omega, the Beginning and the End. He is the Eternal God, the second person of the holy trinity and He is the only way, the truth and the life. (John 14:6 "For unto us a child is born, unto us a son is given: and the government shall be upon his shoulder: and his name shall be called Wonderful, Counsellor, The mighty God, The everlasting Father, The Prince of Peace." (Isaiah 9:6) Apostle John said; "I am Alpha and Omega, the beginning and the ending, saith the Lord, which is, and which was, and which is to come, the Almighty." (Revelation 1:8)

MONDAY
WHY JESUS CHRIST WAS UNIQUE
(Luke 2: 7) "And she brought forth her firstborn son, and wrapped him in swaddling clothes, and laid him in a manger; because there was no room for them in the inn."

Jesus was Born with a Unique Birth. His birth was first mentioned by the Lord Himself in (Genesis 3:15) "And I will put enmity between thee and the woman, and between thy seed and her seed; it shall bruise thy head, and thou shalt bruise his heel." It was the first prophecy in the Bible from the mouth of God. It was the first promised of a Redeemer, a Savior. The place of His birth was also prophesied in (Micah 5: 2) His birth was prophesied by both major and minor prophets hundreds of years before he was born. His birth was unique.

Jesus was a Man with a Unique Life. (John 8:46). He was completely man but He was sinless. His works and ministry was unique. He heals and raised Lazarus from the dead. "He taketh away the sins of the world". And He loves us in spite of our sinfulness. He cares for us and did miracles and still performing miracles. Jesus influenced the world from the time He was born until this present times and the time to come.

Jesus was a Man with Unique Words. He spoke in parables, He rebuke people with love and compassion. He spoke with power. He caused the blind to see... He raised the dead... and took control of the nature with His Words. (Luke 21: 33). The devil trembles at His Word. We sing His Words and we write songs, hymns, poems and quotes His Words. We get encouragement and convicted of our sins by His Words.

Jesus was a Man with Unique Death. He died not for Himself, but for us, for our sins. He died for the salvation of mankind. He died to give us hope. He died so we can live. He died, He was buried and rose again the third day according to the Scriptures and He's coming back.

Jesus is Unique Because He is a King, but was Born in a Manger. He created the world but he did not own a home when he was here on earth. "And Jesus said unto him, Foxes have holes, and birds of the air have nests; but the Son of man hath not where to lay his head." (Luke 9: 58) He was rich but He became poor. He owns the cattle of the thousand hills, but he was buried in a borrowed tomb. The Father said; "For every beast of the forest is mine, and the cattle upon a thousand hills." He is the King of kings and Lord of lords, but He was the Servant of men. (Philippians 2: 5- 7) 5- "Let this mind be in you, which was also in Christ Jesus: 6- Who, being in the form of God, thought it not robbery to be equal with God: 7- But made himself of no reputation, and took upon him the form of a servant, and was made in the likeness of men:" (Psalms 50:10) He came down and humbled Himself to love, but he was hated even of His own. But one thing for sure… and this will never change… "His name is JESUS, for He will save His people from their sins." "21- And she shall bring forth a son, and thou shalt call his name JESUS: for he shall save his people from their sins. 22- Now all this was done, that it might be fulfilled which was spoken of the Lord by the prophet, saying, 23- Behold, a virgin shall be with child, and shall bring forth a son, and they shall call his name Emmanuel, which being interpreted is, God with us. 24- Then Joseph being raised from sleep did as the angel of the Lord had bidden him, and took unto him his wife: 25- And knew her not till she had brought forth her firstborn son: and he called his name JESUS." (Matthew 1:21- 25) He can be yours today just ask Him (Jesus) to come into your heart. And make this Christmas a meaningful and memorable one.

TUESDAY

7 THINGS TO HELP YOU STEP UP TO THE NEXT LEVEL

(Philippians 3:13- 16) "13- Brethren, I count not myself to have apprehended: but this one thing I do, forgetting those things which are behind, and reaching forth unto those things which are before, 14- I press toward the mark for the prize of the high calling of God in Christ Jesus. 15- Let us therefore, as many as be perfect, be thus minded: and if in anything ye be otherwise minded, God shall reveal even this unto you. 16- Nevertheless, whereto we have already attained, let us walk by the same rule, let us mind the same thing."

During the start of the New Year; people all over the world has some kind of formula and New Year's resolution as they look forward to the success of their business, in their family circle, good health as well as for their future. But seldom will you hear and see people seeking the truth of the Bible and learning or leaning on the leading of the Holy Spirit of God. Notice the 7 THINGS TO HELP YOU STEP UP TO THE NEXT LEVEL:

1- *Learn from Your Past...* "He who does not learn from history will repeat the same..." Read (Philippians 3).
2- *Forget About the Past...* failures, heartache, hurt, hopelessness. Don't live on your past, look forward, stay focus and maintain your momentum. 14- "I press toward the mark for the prize of the high calling of God in Christ Jesus."
3- *Know Your Present Standing or Condition.* Know your financial, spiritual, physical, emotional and your intellectual conditions. Don't live in denial and excuses. (Philippians 3:15- 16)
4- *Know Your Goal.* What do you really want to accomplish this year and in the future. Do you have a short term and long term goals? Check on (Philippians 3:12- 14)
5- *Be Determined to Accomplish or Reach Those Goals.* It may not be easy but remember the sayings, "NO PAIN, NO GAIN". It's true indeed; if you don't have patience in anything you do, you will never gain... not even a step higher to the next level. (Philippians 3:12- 14)

6- *Let God Leads You.* "1- The LORD is my shepherd; I shall not want. 2- He maketh me to lie down in green pastures: he leadeth me beside the still waters." (Psalms 23:1- 2)

7- *Don't Forget God as You Prosper and Successful.* "8- This book of the law shall not depart out of thy mouth; but thou shalt meditate therein day and night, that thou mayest observe to do according to all that is written therein: for then thou shalt make thy way prosperous, and then thou shalt have good success. 13- Remember the word which Moses the servant of the LORD commanded you, saying, The LORD your God hath given you rest, and hath given you this land." (Joshua 1:8; 13) God bless you and HAVE A BLESSED AND PROSPEROUS NEW YEAR!!!

WEDNESDAY
"FORGIVENESS AND FORGETTING..."

(Psalm 103:10- 12) "He hath not dealt with us after our sins; nor rewarded us according to our iniquities. 11- For as the heaven is high above the earth, so great is his mercy toward them that fear him. 12- As far as the east is from the west, so far hath he removed our transgressions from us."

Forgiveness is overcoming by love the sin, mistakes, fault of the other party without any condition or resentment. Dr. Billy Graham wrote; "When we come to Christ, God imparts His righteousness to us. It is as if an accounting entry had been made in the books in heaven, declaring us righteous for Christ's sake. The Divine Bookkeeper cancels our debt!" (Hope for Each Day April 14, "Forgiveness and Fellowship") The Bible says; "Wherefore I say unto thee, Her sins, which are many, are forgiven; for she loved much: but to whom little is forgiven, the same loveth little. 48- And he said unto her, Thy sins are forgiven." (Luke 7:47- 48) There was a sticker in a car which says; "IF YOU THINK YOU'RE PERFECT, TRY WALKING ON THE WATER!" and the other one said; "Christians are not perfect, they're just forgiven". It is true indeed. Apostle Paul wrote; "31- Let all bitterness, and wrath, and anger, and clamour, and evil speaking, be put away from you, with all malice: 32- And be ye kind one to another, tenderhearted, forgiving one another, even as God for Christ's sake hath forgiven you." (Ephesians 4:31- 32)

You cannot serve God and offer Him your best service and at the same time you are holding a grudge, you hated someone or you have resentment in your heart. You have to settle it down at the altar of forgiveness and you let the shed blood of the Lord Jesus Christ cleanse you for whatever sin you have in your heart. Forgiveness is dropping off all your baggage behind you in the ocean of love- the love of God, and not to be taken back forever and ever. Millions of people are living with baggage and in sins and with bitterness. You cannot have an unforgiving spirit, gossip, anger and wrath in your life and expect God to bless you! I understand that what happened in the past; the pain and the hurt that you went through will never be erased in your sub-conscious mind, but you can bury those sins in the blood of the Lord Jesus Christ and in His death, burial and resurrection. It's either you will erase it by His grace or you will be erased by it. I made a song out of this verse when I was a new Christian a long time ago. It's a beautiful and very powerful verse from the Scriptures about repentance and forgiveness. "Repent therefore of this thy wickedness, and pray God, if perhaps the thought of thine heart may be forgiven thee."(I John 1:9) "If we confess our sins, he is faithful and just to forgive us our sins, and to cleanse us from all unrighteousness." (Acts 8:22)

THURSDAY

CHRIST'S RICHES IS WAY BETTER THAN THE TREASURES IN EGYPT

(Hebrews 11:25- 26) "25- Choosing rather to suffer affliction with the people of God, than to enjoy the pleasures of sin for a season; 26- Esteeming the reproach of Christ greater riches than the treasures in Egypt: for he had respect unto the recompense of the reward."

Here's a good comparison of what life would be with Moses in Egypt along with Christ and the children of Israel together with Pharaoh and his people (the Egyptians)

*Moses in Egypt with Christ and the Children of Israel:*1- He was called the son of God. 2- He was living by faith. 3- He was not afraid of the king's commandment, he believed on the commandments of God. 4- He refused to be called: a) - Son of Pharaoh's daughter, b)- As the master of the Egyptians. c) - One of the taskmasters of the Egyptians, but would rather be a servant. 5- He was not afraid of the wrath of the king. 6- He sees the future and the One who holds the future. Moses was living in the spirit and not in the flesh. He is living in the riches of the King of kings. 7- He saw Christ on His throne... 8- He kept the Passover and exercised his faith... 9- He was used by the Lord as an instrument of God's miracle...

Moses in Egypt with Pharaoh and the Mixed Multitude: 1- He was called "the son of Pharaoh's daughter". 2- He was living by sight and not by faith. 3- He was living under the iron hands of Pharaoh and under Pharaoh's command. 4- He was the "the son of Pharaoh's daughter"; the taskmaster of the people and he was not a servant, but a prince. 5- He was living in fear. 6- He was living in the flesh and living in the riches of the king. 7- He was always looking on Pharaoh and on his throne. 8- He kept Pharaoh's religion and religious activities as he served the gods of Pharaoh. 9- He was used by Pharaoh as an instrument of his godless, vicious and selfish dreams. 10- He became a leader of the Egyptians. 11- He was a leader of a godless nation and people. Compare (Exodus chapters 1- 3 with Hebrews 11:23- 29). The writer of the book of Hebrews said; "3- For every high priest is ordained to offer gifts and sacrifices: wherefore it is of necessity that this man have somewhat also to offer. 4- For if he were on earth, he should not be a priest, seeing that there are priests that offer gifts according to the law: 5- Who serve unto the example and shadow of heavenly things, as Moses was admonished of God when he was about to make the tabernacle: for, See, saith he, that thou make all things according to the pattern showed to thee in the mount." (Hebrews 8:3- 5)

FRIDAY

WINNING BY FAITH WITH THE LORD ON YOUR SIDE

(Hebrews 11:3) "Through faith we understand that the worlds were framed by the word of God, so that things which are seen were not made of things which do appear."

The Bible is the mirror of everyone from the least to the greatest. During the time of Moses, they don't have the whole Scriptures. Notice what the New Testament was saying about faith, vision, suffering for the sake of the Lord Jesus Christ. We must also consider the potential that we have in Him as we stand by His side (Hebrews 11:24). People who have a different perspective, different outlook in life and different dreams and vision might think that Moses was crazy. He turned his back from the pleasures of the world. You may have heard your friends and love ones said something negative against you and against your decision for Christ when you trade the pleasures of this world for Christ. People who turned their back from the good offer of the world, the great perks and a big chunk of money in exchanged for the Name of Christ were called crazy, out of their minds or silly for rejecting something that is valuable to many. According to Matthew Henry; "Faith and hope go together; and the same things that are the object of our hope are the object of our faith. It is a firm persuasion and expectation that God will perform all that he has promised to us in Christ; and this persuasion is so strong that it gives the soul a kind of possession and present fruition of those things, gives them a subsistence in the soul, by the first-fruits and foretastes of them: so that believers in the exercise of faith are filled with joy unspeakable and full of glory. Christ dwells in the soul by faith, and the soul is filled with the fullness of God, as far as his present measure will admit; he experiences a substantial reality in the objects of faith." (The Bible Collection, Matthew Henry) The Lord promised us of what He will do for us by our faith or if we step by faith, but we also have to use our resources, potential and sometimes hard work. "Faith without work is dead..." says James.

At the start of the year, I make it a point and try to finish reading the book of Dr. John C. Maxwell- "Think on These Things" Mr. Maxwell said, "The people who constantly rise to the top are those who possess a vision before the prize is won. They see the triumph before anyone else. During times of discouragement, they pursue the dream while others criticize, they continue striving. They push aside the problems and point to the potential. They behave like victors before the contest. Why? Because they've already seen the victory in their mind." Yes, I believe that they've already seen the victory in the future right in their minds. The people during Moses' times might have thought that Moses was out of his mind when he refused to be called Pharaoh's daughter. Moses did not hold on to the position that he has and will have in the future. He also refused the power that was already in his hand and more power if he stayed in the palace during those times. He also refused the great provisions and pleasures the palace could offer... instead he ends up tending the sheep and became a servant. The Bible said; "Esteeming the reproach of Christ greater riches than the treasures in Egypt: for he had respect unto the recompense of the reward." (Hebrews 11:26)

SATURDAY

THE FAITH THAT SEES THE FUTURE

(Hebrews 11:1- 2) "1- Now faith is the substance of things hoped for, the evidence of things not seen. 2- For by it the elders obtained a good report."

The parents of Moses did not have any idea about these verses, but they actually put these verses into practiced when they hid him and made a decision that could endanger both their life and Moses' life. When the parents of Moses hid him, it was actually an act of faith on their part. It may sound like they don't care, but during those times when the enemies were after the babies and little kids; it was of necessities on their part. When they hid him, they hid him from the enemies but God has a purpose. "23- By faith Moses, when he was born, was hid three months of his parents, because they saw he was a proper child; and they were not afraid of the king's commandment. 24- By faith Moses, when he was come to years, refused to be called the son of Pharaoh's daughter;" (Hebrews 11:23- 24) It was almost the same scenario when Jesus was born in Bethlehem and King Herod was running after him. King Herod was trying to kill the 2 years old and below and most especially the Lord Jesus Christ. It's not the "Hocus Pocus of the magicians and all the tricks of the card readers that can make you see what God can do to the future. The prophet Habakkuk called it "the vision from God". The book of Proverbs said; "Where there is no vision, the people perish."

Moses was the picture of the Lord Jesus Christ in the Old Testament. In (Exodus 2:2) "And the woman conceived, and bare a son: and when she saw him that he was a goodly child, she hid him three months." It was a great discernment on Moses' parents. They were looking on Moses the way God see him. I believe that the stronger your faith, the greater and the more you're sensitive to God's leading and also the more God will give you the discernment. Few years ago; I was looking to a little kid and I was observing him… In my mind, I was thinking that that kid was smart and he would grow smart. He is now a teenager and he is very smart. One of my friends met this kid in one of the party that we attended and he said the same thing- the kid is smart. Jesus can tame the nature and He can do whatever seems impossible in the eyes of man. He is the God of the possible and the impossible. There was a song which says, "I never prayed like this before, for I'm asking you, not to close the door, for I can tame the wind and still the water, if you just let me..." I believe that Jesus can tame the wind and still the water even if it is against our will. Jesus controls everything. It means that this should encourage us to look at the future in the eyes of faith and in a positive way. Let us look at the future with the right perspective. The Bible said; "19- Thy way is in the sea, and thy path in the great waters, and thy footsteps are not known. 5- Trust in the LORD with all thine heart; and lean not unto thine own understanding. 6- In all thy ways acknowledge him, and he shall direct thy paths." (Psalm 77:19; Proverbs 3:5- 6) Jesus and the Apostles recognized the power of God and the wisdom of God in Moses' life. "22- And Moses was learned in all the wisdom of the Egyptians, and was mighty in words and in deeds. 23- And when he was full forty years old, it came into his heart to visit his brethren the children of Israel. 24- And seeing one of them suffer wrong, he defended him, and avenged him that was oppressed, and smote the Egyptian: 25- For he supposed his brethren would have understood how that God by his hand would deliver them: but they understood not." (Acts 7:22- 25)

SUNDAY
IT WAS BY FAITH...

(Hebrews 11:24- 26) "24- By faith Moses, when he was come to years, refused to be called the son of Pharaoh's daughter; 25- Choosing rather to suffer affliction with the people of God, than to enjoy the pleasures of sin for a season; 26- Esteeming the reproach of Christ greater riches than the treasures in Egypt: for he had respect unto the recompense of the reward."

Dr. Jerry Falwell said; "In spite of all our mistakes, shortcomings, weaknesses and vices, if we can learn how to live by faith, we will overcome everything else. We will achieve our goals in victorious living." "Faith means holding on to God right to the last moment, knowing He will never let you down." We have weak homes because we have weak faith and conviction. There are those who live in abundance, but they are living without God, without love and without faith in their homes. Someone said, "Faith is making real what cannot be seen or sensed with our human faculties." Some Christians are almost immune of the word 'faith' already that some of them could not even appreciate and practice it in their daily walk with the Lord. Faith is not what you think or feel in whatever situation you are in right now and what you have inside of you... You exercise that faith by letting the Holy Spirit of God work in you and through you. You have to claim what God has promised in His Word. It was not easy for Moses who was so wealthy, powerful and very dependent to his (so called) parents and to the riches of Egypt. I believe that God used Moses' influence, his family background and his personality to help the Israelites get out of the land of Egypt. Whatever happened to the children of Israel as they stepped out of Egypt was because of the faith of Moses to God. The Lord has worked miraculously in him and through him. It was not part of the cycle of life, but it was God who promised him of His presence. Moses was born in a family who believed in God and he grew up under the power and the influenced of the king. It's so easy to live with what you have in your hand or in your reach, but it's so different when you don't see anything and don't feel anything. We used to sing this song in my youth group:

> "I just keep trusting my Lord, as I walk alone.
> I just keep trusting the Lord, and He gave me a song..."

I was inspired to wrote this short poems while I was thinking of God's love, our hope and faith in Him...

> "The love of God was Christ's manifestation,
> He shared at the cross of Calvary;
> The angels cannot contend the emotions,
> As Christ was dying on the cross to end man's chains
> The love so strong, the hell was shaken,
> Because of His love we were forgiven;
> The rich and poor or the miserable
> Find hope in God through faith we've taken"- ERS

If all you see are dark clouds and dark paths, putting your trust in God should be your next step. "By faith Moses, when he was born, was hid three months of his parents, because they saw he was a proper child; and they were not afraid of the king's commandment. 27- By faith he forsook Egypt, not fearing the wrath of the king: for he endured, as seeing him who is invisible." (Hebrews 11:23; 27)

MONDAY

GOD'S UNCONDITIONAL LOVE…

(John 10:15; 17- 18) "15- As the Father knoweth me, even so know I the Father: and I lay down my life for the sheep. 17- Therefore doth my Father love me, because I lay down my life, that I might take it again.18- No man taketh it from me, but I lay it down of myself. I have power to lay it down, and I have power to take it again. This commandment have I received of my Father."

Henry Ward Beecher said; "Love is the river of life in this world." According to Sir James M. Barrie; "If you have it, you don't need to have anything else. And if you don't have it, it doesn't matter what else you have." Sirs Paul McCartney and John Lennon song; "Love is all you need." In Romans chapter five verses five to ten; you will notice 2 things: *a) Man's conditions* in verse 6 and *b) The Messiah's Comfort.*

Man's Condition: "We were without strength…" It means we are unworthy, nothing, weak, like a dried fig tree. Let us picture ourselves buried in a dirt, neck deep. We are dead in sins and trespasses according to Apostle Paul in (Ephesians 2:1- 5). We were "ungodly"- It means we were under the power of the darkness of this world. We were servants of sin. We live under the control of lusts, worldly pleasures, under the prince of the power of this world, we were disobedient and the children of wrath. But the *Messiah's Comfort* is that He died for us. Christ died for the ungodly, for sinners like you and me. It was His love that put Him on the cross. It was His death that made us worthy of His love, His heaven, His salvation and His throne. What a comfort and privileges that we have in Christ. This brief outline will tell us of the His riches of His love. It's about the unconditional *Love of God.*

- God the Father, Because of His Great Love for Us, He Gave us His Only Begotten Son. (John 3:16)

- Θεσυσ Γαϖε Ηισ Λιφε φορ Υσ. (Θοην 15: 9–14)

- He Give Us this Life and Eternal Life in Heaven. (I John 5:10- 15)

- God Forgave Us of Our Sins. (I John 1:8- 9)

> Jesus is the Shepherd from a manger
> God sent Him to die for sinner;
> He sacrifice to please the Father
> For Him alone and there's no other- ERS

Frederick M. Lehman wrote; "The Love of God is greater far than tongue or pen can ever tell, It goes beyond the highest star; And reaches to the lowest hell..."

What more can we ask from the God who created us and opened His *heart* and *home* in *heaven* for us. "But God, who is rich in mercy, for his great love wherewith he loved us, 5- Even when we were dead in sins, hath quickened us together with Christ, (by grace ye are saved;)- And hath raised us up together, and made us sit together in heavenly places in Christ Jesus:" (Ephesians 2:4- 6)

TUESDAY
FAITH THAT WORKS!!!

(Ephesians 2:7- 10) "7- That in the ages to come he might show the exceeding riches of his grace in his kindness toward us through Christ Jesus. 8- For by grace are ye saved through faith; and that not of yourselves: it is the gift of God: 9- Not of works, lest any man should boast. 10- For we are his workmanship, created in Christ Jesus unto good works, which God hath before ordained that we should walk in them."

Matthew Henry wrote; "1. Negatively: Not of yourselves, v. 8. Our faith, our conversion, and our eternal salvation, are not the mere product of any natural abilities, nor of any merit of our own: Not of works, lest any man should boast, v. 9. These things are not brought to pass by anything done by us, and therefore all boasting is excluded; he who glories must not glory in himself, but in the Lord. There is no room for any man's boasting of his own abilities and power; or as though he had done anything that might deserve such immense favours from God. 2. Positively: But God, who is rich in mercy, etc., v. 4. God himself is the author of this great and happy change, and his great love is the spring and fontal cause of it; hence he resolved to show mercy. Love is his inclination to do us good considered simply as creatures; mercy respects us as apostate and as miserable creatures. Observe, God's eternal love or good-will towards his creatures is the fountain whence all his mercies vouch-safed to us proceed; and that love of God is great love, and that mercy of his is rich mercy, inexpressibly great and inexhaustibly rich." (The Bible Collection, by, Matthew Henry)

Amazing Grace is a very popular song which touched millions of lives:

"Amazing Grace, how sweet the sound,
That saved a wretch like me.
I once was lost but now am found,
Was blind, but now I see.
T'was Grace that taught my heart to fear.
And Grace, my fears relieved.
How precious did that Grace appear
The hour I first believed.
Through many dangers, toils and snares
I have already come;
'Tis Grace that brought me safe thus far
and Grace will lead me home.
When we've been there, ten thousand years
Bright shining as the sun,
We've no less days to sing God's praise
Than when we've first begun.
(John Newton 1725- 1807)

"4- But God, who is rich in mercy, for his great love wherewith he loved us, 5- Even when we were dead in sins, hath quickened us together with Christ, (by grace ye are saved;)" (Ephesians 2:4- 5)

WEDNESDAY

GOD'S MIRACULOUS OPERATIONS THROUGH FAITH

(Hebrews 11:32- 34) "32- And what shall I more say? for the time would fail me to tell of Gedeon, and of Barak, and of Samson, and of Jephthae; of David also, and Samuel, and of the prophets: 33- Who through faith subdued kingdoms, wrought righteousness, obtained promises, stopped the mouths of lions, 34- Quenched the violence of fire, escaped the edge of the sword, out of weakness were made strong, waxed valiant in fight, turned to flight the armies of the aliens."

God has not changed and will never change! He is the same yesterday, today and tomorrow. God's principles will not change, but his method and His way of working miracles and showing His power varies from time to time. His dealings with people from different places and events may be different, but His character will still be the same and His power to work miracles in and through us will always stand strong. Notice *God's Principles of Operations* in "9- And she said unto the men, I know that the LORD hath given you the land, and that your terror is fallen upon us, and that all the inhabitants of the land faint because of you. 10- For we have heard how the LORD dried up the water of the Red sea for you, when ye came out of Egypt; and what ye did unto the two kings of the Amorites, that were on the other side Jordan, Sihon and Og, whom ye utterly destroyed. 11- And as soon as we had heard these things, our hearts did melt, neither did there remain any more courage in any man, because of you: for the LORD your God, he is God in heaven above, and in earth beneath." (Joshua 2:9- 11) Here's my personal view of how the Lord operates and why He performs miracles and show His power in us and through us. First, God revealed to us His promises in the Scriptures. Secondly, God will initiate His purpose. Thirdly, He is preparing others or the people around you to witness that miracle or blessings. His promised is fulfilled in you and through you. Also, notice *God's People in the Lord's Operations...* (Joshua 2:3; 9- 11; 3:15- 17) But in (Joshua 1:17) "According as we hearkened unto Moses in all things, so will we hearken unto thee: only the LORD thy God be with thee, as he was with Moses." The Israelites were there waiting and willing to "GO" "OBEY" "STEP OUT OF THEIR COMFORT ZONE" and "LISTEN". The lessons to learn are; God will not work in His church if there is envy, jealousy, disunity or division, selfishness and pride. They (the Israelites) during the time of Joshua stood in unity for the Lord and His purpose. *The Lord's Power is in Operation and Demonstrated through His Children.* People will call you a fool, fanatic and other names because you put God first in your life and you identify yourself with the Lord Jesus Christ. Is it foolishness, fanaticism or faithfulness when you refused to work on Sundays and refused double pay, because you have to be in church for worship? (Matthew 6:33). You stand for what is right and for the truth. You say *NO* to sin, Satan and self gratification. Will you call it foolishness, religious fanatics or faithfulness to a loving God? We trust God in every aspects of life; it means in everything because we know He is faithful and we want to remain faithful to Him. Gideon was a man who has no self worth and self esteem. He was used by the Lord because in spite of his personal issues, he trusted the Lord as he obeyed God.

In (Mark 12:24) "And Jesus answering said unto them, Do ye not therefore err, because ye know not the scriptures, neither the power of God? Wow! That was a very powerful question and statement. Apostle Paul wrote; "3- Since ye seek a proof of Christ speaking in me, which to you-ward is not weak, but is mighty in you. 4- For though he was crucified through weakness, yet he liveth by the power of God. For we also are weak in him, but we shall live with him by the power of God toward you. 5- Examine yourselves, whether ye be in the faith; prove your own selves. Know ye not your own selves, how that Jesus Christ is in you, except ye be reprobates?" (II Corinthians 13:3- 5)

THURSDAY

THE FAITH OF A BORDERLINE BELIEVER

(Joshua 14:11- 12) "11- As yet I am as strong this day as I was in the day that Moses sent me: as my strength was then, even so is my strength now, for war, both to go out, and to come in. 12- Now therefore give me this mountain, whereof the LORD spake in that day; for thou heardest in that day how the Anakims were there, and that the cities were great and fenced: if so be the LORD will be with me, then I shall be able to drive them out, as the LORD said."

What is a borderline? The definition of *borderline* as according to Webster dictionary: "A line that establishes or marks a border. 2. An indefinite area intermediate between two qualities or conditions: The borderline between love and hate is often thin. adj.1. a. Verging on a given quality or condition: borderline poverty. b. Of a questionable nature or quality: an applicant with borderline qualifications.2. a. Psychology Relating to any phenomenon that is intermediate between two groups and not clearly categorized in either group: a borderline state showing the characteristics of both neurotic and psychotic reactions. b. Relating to a condition characterized by a pattern of instability in mood, interpersonal relations, and self-image, and manifested by self-destructive, impulsive, and inconsistent behavior: the borderline syndrome.

With just the definition of the word *"borderline"*; we can already picture in our minds what kind of faith does the borderline Christians has. There are Christians who claimed to be faithful or they claimed to be serving the Lord; but they don't want to go all the way with the Lord and His Word. The example of the children of Gad, Reuben and Manasseh is an excellent picture of the believers who lives beyond their borderline. "25- And the children of Gad and the children of Reuben spake unto Moses, saying, Thy servants will do as my lord commandeth. 26- Our little ones, our wives, our flocks, and all our cattle, shall be there in the cities of Gilead: 27- But thy servants will pass over, every man armed for war, before the LORD to battle, as my lord saith. 30- But if they will not pass over with you armed, they shall have possessions among you in the land of Canaan. 31- And the children of Gad and the children of Reuben answered, saying, As the LORD hath said unto thy servants, so will we do. 32- We will pass over armed before the LORD into the land of Canaan, that the possession of our inheritance on this side Jordan may be ours." (Numbers 32:25- 27; 30- 32) We need Christians who could say and do the things, like what Gad and Reuben did in the presence of Moses and of God. (25). Notice, in verse 26, they also made their love ones follow after them which is a good example of a family who are united for the service of our King. In verse 27, we see here not only their courage to go forward for the Lord and to fight in the name and for the name of God, but also for the faith in which they stood for. They did not hesitate, they were single minded, they were not impulsive or inconsistent with their stand, and they were focus. Joshua chapter fourteen is a good example about stepping out of our borderline as we exercise our faith. The faith of the borderline Christians are not as the same as those who really have faith in God. I'm talking about the Christians who are really active and working not only for them, but also for the work of the Lord. (Joshua 3:15- 17) The borderline Christians is like a wave says Apostle James. They're unstable and weak. "But let him ask in faith, nothing wavering. For he that wavereth is like a wave of the sea driven with the wind and tossed." (James 1:6)

FRIDAY

GOD IS THE MAIN FOCUS OF FAITH

(Hebrews 11:6) "But without faith it is impossible to please him: for he that cometh to God must believe that he is, and that he is a rewarder of them that diligently seek him."

Joshua chapters 10 and 11 demonstrate a good picture of faith in God. There's no other object of faith, but God. Faith in faith is not the object of our faith, but God is. You cannot have faith in something but in God. When Joshua put his trust in God, he did not have faith in faith, but faith in God who promised him. And just to give us a little background of the events and a brief story on how Joshua ends up fighting with the multitude. In verse 1- Jabin king of Hazor heard about the victory of Joshua against his enemies as according to chapter ten. It is very clear that Joshua was celebrating his victory over the 3 kings in (Joshua 10:39) it says; "And he took it, and the king thereof, and all the cities thereof; and they smote them with the edge of the sword, and utterly destroyed all the souls that were therein; he left none remaining: as he had done to Hebron, so he did to Debir, and to the king thereof; as he had done also to Libnah, and to her king." And because of what he did to those kings, another king tried to step out against Joshua and the children of Israel. Joshua's faith in God comes along with his obedience to God's Word and commands. I believe that the heart of the passages from the Bible verses are the Lord's instructions and the Lord's promised in which He fulfilled when Joshua obeyed by faith. "6- And the LORD said unto Joshua, Be not afraid because of them: for tomorrow about this time will I deliver them up all slain before Israel: thou shalt hock their horses, and burn their chariots with fire. 7- So Joshua came, and all the people of war with him, against them by the waters of Merom suddenly; and they fell upon them. 8- And the LORD delivered them into the hand of Israel, who smote them, and chased them unto great Zidon, and unto Misrephothmaim, and unto the valley of Mizpeh eastward; and they smote them, until they left them none remaining." (Joshua 11:6- 9) It's so easy for us

Christians to be driven away by our emotion, intellectual ideas and selfish motives, when we can just lay everything down in the feet of Jesus at the throne of grace. May we all have the same spirit like the Israelites of old when they said to Joshua; "All that thou commandest us we will do, and whithersoever thou sendest us, we will go." (Joshua 1:16) The Lord said to Joshua; "Be not afraid..." so Joshua went and fought against the enemies of God and the Lord delivered them. Faith in God does not work like a vending machine where you drop some coins, you make a selection, push the buttons and what you want or what you choose will just drop down for you to pick up. Faith in God is more of God working in you, through the power of the Holy Spirit. You response according to His will, according to His Word and you obey His voice. You really have to believe that God knows what He is doing, He knows what lies ahead, and He knows our future. Let me give you one of my definitions of faith; "Faith is dropping everything from off your hands and your life and entrusting them to God, knowing that He is in control."

Notice what Paul said; "So then faith cometh by hearing, and hearing by the word of God." (Romans 10:17)

SATURDAY

DON'T CHARGE, LET GOD BE IN CHARGE

(Philippians 4:13) "I can do all things through Christ which strengtheneth me."

My son Eliezer started a business called Music Prescription. The main reasons why he started the business are: 1- To honor and glorify the Lord. 2- To minister effectively through music. 3- To be legitimate in the music business… Although not everyone likes the idea on what he's doing but we have seen people came to know the Lord through his ministry. Recently Music Prescription along with International Community Christian Church and First Baptist Church both from Trenton, Michigan with other businesses sponsored a concert for Jaci Velasquez and Eliel Lyn and the Band. One of my favorite songs by Jaci Velasquez reminds me of God being in charge: "As long as stars shine down from heaven, And the rivers run into the sea 'til the end of time forever… And I will never leave you, I need you."

This is happening every day and in the whole world as people keep on doing everything with their own strength and power and they put everything in their own hands. And it's a cycle, because at the end of our rope… we will end up turning up our head to God, and down on our knees in prayer. And we will end up putting our trust in Him and let Him finish and clean up our messed. If you would just think of how life would look like without Jesus and without His love. He is the one who set us free from doubt, self- sufficiency and sins. He will still be in charge of everything including those that we put the charged on in our plastic. Jesus said; "4 Abide in me, and I in you. As the branch cannot bear fruit of itself, except it abide in the vine; no more can ye, except ye abide in me. 5- I am the vine, ye are the branches: He that abideth in me, and I in him, the same bringeth forth much fruit: for without me ye can do nothing." (John 15:4- 5)

According to The Bible Collection on Henry Complete Commentary; Mr. Matthew Henry wrote regarding (Philippians 4:19). He said; "He does as it were draw a bill upon the exchequer in heaven, and leaves it to God to make them amends for the kindness they had shown him. He shall do it, not only as your God, but as my God, who takes what is done to me as done to himself. You supplied my needs, according to your poverty; and he shall supply yours, according to his riches." But still it is by Christ Jesus; through him we have grace to do that which is good, and through him we must expect the reward of it. Not of debt, but of grace; for the more we do for God the more we are indebted to him, because we receive the more from him." "Then he answered and spake unto me, saying, This is the word of the LORD unto Zerubbabel, saying, Not by might, nor by power, but by my spirit, saith the LORD of hosts." (Zechariah 4:6)

SUNDAY
"GOD IS IN CHARGE"

(Exodus 31:3) "And I have filled him with the spirit of God, in wisdom, and in understanding, and in knowledge, and in all manner of workmanship,"

God is the one who empowers His servants for His service and glory. God is the one who empowers us and gives us the grace and the wisdom as we serve Him and minister in His name and for His glory. Even from the least and little detail God is into it. God is looking for people who is willing to do right.

God's Will for Us is to be Commitment Driven Church or Christians. A church or Christians must be willing to take the responsibilities for God. A church must be willing to make decisions based on the principles of the Word of God. "And thou shalt speak unto all that are wise hearted, whom I have filled with the spirit of wisdom, that they may make Aaron's garments to consecrate him, that he may minister unto me in the priest's office." (Exodus 31: 3) "And I have filled him with the spirit of God, in wisdom, and in understanding, and in knowledge, and in all manner of workmanship," (Exodus 28:3) God provides not just the spiritual but the mental, physical and other needs to finish the job or so His ministry can go through.

When God Gives You the Vision, it will come with His Provision. "And I, behold, I have given with him Aholiab, the son of Ahisamach, of the tribe of Dan: and in the hearts of all that are wise hearted I have put wisdom, that they may make all that I have commanded thee;" (Exodus 31:6) Even in our preaching and teaching, we are able to share His Word with power and conviction because of the working of the Holy Spirit of God. So don't take the glory from that good preaching or teaching that you have or you will have. The glory belongs to God. (Numbers 11:25; 29) Maintain that momentum for God. Continue serving the Lord even in the midst of problems. Be steady... in verse "29- And Moses said unto him, Enviest thou for my sake? Would God that all the LORD'S people were prophets, and that the LORD would put his spirit upon them!" We need to have the right attitude. The actions and reaction we make must be controlled by the Holy Spirit and must be controlled with our right attitude. (Judges 11: 29) Even with the physical strength that we need… we need to do what we're supposed to do for God. He is in charge. He did it to Samson and He can do the same to you. We can see in these verses that God is in charge; "3- Every place that the sole of your foot shall tread upon, that have I given unto you, as I said unto Moses. 4- From the wilderness and this Lebanon even unto the great river, the river Euphrates, all the land of the Hittites, and unto the great sea toward the going down of the sun, shall be your coast. 5- There shall not any man be able to stand before thee all the days of thy life: as I was with Moses, so I will be with thee: I will not fail thee, nor forsake thee. 6- There shall not any man be able to stand before thee all the days of thy life: as I was with Moses, so I will be with thee: I will not fail thee, nor forsake thee." (Joshua 1:3- 6)

MONDAY
FAITH OF OUR FATHERS

(Hebrews 11:29- 31) "29- By faith they passed through the Red sea as by dry land: which the Egyptians assaying to do were drowned. 30- By faith the walls of Jericho fell down, after they were compassed about seven days. 31- By faith the harlot Rahab perished not with them that believed not, when she had received the spies with peace."

God gave us so many things and He gave things to people that cannot be numbered. Time and even our limited minds cannot fathom the goodness, the blessings and the things that He gave us as His children. God had given so many things to the children of Israel even before they crossed over the Jordan River to enter the promise land. As believers, we must step forward towards God given goals and blessings in our lives, especially in our spiritual lives. We have to claim it for God, for ourselves and for His honor. *(Joshua 1:3; 8- 9)* Apostle Paul wrote these while in prison; "4- Be careful for nothing; but in everything by prayer and supplication with thanksgiving let your requests be made known unto God. 19- But my God shall supply all your need according to his riches in glory by Christ Jesus." (Philippians 4:6, 19) Someone asked me one day, he said; "How come we don't have the miracles that God was doing during the Old and New Testament times like the parting of the Red sea, the parting of the Jordan River, the feeding of the 5,000 and many others..." And I replied; "Because we don't have the faith, the love and commitment that they have during their times." God has not changed and He will never change, but Christians have changed dramatically. We have changed in terms of how we treated the Word of God. We have changed with how we treated and valued God and Christianity. Church activities and other religious ritual and activities are more of a friendship building and relationship building instead of evangelistic focus or evangelistic centered activities.

Our love for God will say more of our faith and dedication for Him. If you love the Lord, your faith and your commitment to God will always follow. There's no difference with your relationship with your spouse or with your love ones. If you love your spouse, you also trust him or her. If you love the Lord, you will put your trust in Him in any circumstances you may have. I wish every believer of the Lord Jesus Christ will exercise their faith not just at church; but at home, at work, in school and in difficult times like these. Esther exercised her faith in such a time as these. When others won't stand for Jesus and are afraid to stand on what the Word of God said... May we all stand up for what is right, moral and pleasing to God. The question should be, "Where is the faith of our fathers like Abraham, Moses, Jacob and Elijah?" It's not, where's God's miracle at... in times like these? It was not easy for Daniel and the 3 Hebrew children to stand up against king Nebuchadnezzar. But we saw God's miracles in their lives because of their faith in God. God is not as interested in our ability and our talents as compared to our trust in Him. May we all put our heart and minds to what God have said in His Word- the Holy Bible. Let us live by faith and not by sight, says the Bible. "Trust in the LORD with all thine heart; and lean not unto thine own understanding. 6- In all thy ways acknowledge him, and he shall direct thy paths." (Proverbs 3:5- 6)

TUESDAY

THE WORLD HAS YET TO SEE, WHAT GOD CAN DO...

(Joshua 1:8) "This book of the law shall not depart out of thy mouth; but thou shalt meditate therein day and night, that thou mayest observe to do according to all that is written therein: for then thou shalt make thy way prosperous, and then thou shalt have good success."

My name is Celso Namuco. I used to be a civic youth leader in our village. I did not come from a political clan or wealthy families, but the Lord called me through this way to get my attention and look up to Him for guidance. I was lost, until one day I came to church for the VBS in Williamsburg Baptist Church in Batangas city, Philippines. I came to know the Lord through pastor Rolly Nolido; who was our teacher in Vacation Bible School at that time. Pastor Nolido asked me if I could come back to the church, which I did. I remember when I was sitting on the chair in the pastor's office crying for joy when pastor Rolly led me to pray and asked the Lord to save me. I accepted Christ as my Lord and Savior on January 8, 1993. Since then, I faithfully attended church. I was baptized at the end of the said month and year. I started to see the need and the passion for a handful of our young people in our church. My pastor encouraged me to lead these young people and to bring more teens to our church in which I had the privileged to be of service. I responded positively and organized our youth group. I sensed that the Lord was calling me to a full time Christian service. I enrolled in the seminary in Manila with the help of our church. After a few years, the Lord opened the door for me to pastor my home church and assisting other churches in Metro Manila. The Lord called me to plant a church in Batangas City where I met my wife who at that time was serving her church as a Sunday school teacher. Now, I am here in the States seeking and looking for the door to open for me as a church planter. To God be the glory!

"...TO A MAN FULLY SURRENDERED TO GOD"
"Then shalt thou understand the fear of the LORD, and find the knowledge of God." (Proverbs 2:5)

My name is VirgilioPansacala, (AKA) Ver. I started my searched for a deeper relationship with God since I was 12 years old. I struggled with the truth that I was a sinner because since childhood, I was good and very religious. My mother influenced me to be a religious kid. I used to serve with my mother in church which I enjoyed very much. One day, I was in the church looking at the cross which leads me to a question; "Am I serving the true God and in the right way?" But while I pondered on that question in my heart, due to the heat and dehydration; I collapsed and when I gained consciousness, I found myself outside the church. That was the last time I visited the church and I started my search for God outside the church. When I was in high school, my classmate gave me a Gideon International New Testament Bible and I started reading it. Then, as I began to realized that my former belief and practiced were totally different to the Lord Jesus Christ's teachings in the New Testament such as the mass, the baptism, the Lord supper, the confession, the prayers and even the Bible itself. In 1979, I found a Baptist church where all the questions in my mind and my searched about the Bible and my belief had come to an end. Because of my self-righteousness I thought, I was already saved but when I was asked where I would be going when I die, I don't have the answer. On that night, I decided to end my self-righteousness. I admitted that I was a sinner and going to hell and I need a Saviour. I repented of my sins and received the Lord Jesus Christ in my heart. There's joy in my heart that I cannot explain when I put my trust in Him. I felt His loving care and never in my life that I felt lonely and empty. Jesus Christ is in me and I claimed His promised that "He will never leave me nor forsake me." I am married to Lucy and we were blessed with 2 God fearing and loving children; Vernon and Bernice. I started a church in Montalban, Rizal when I was in my early years in the Seminary in International Baptist Theological College in the

Philippines. I started a church in Whitley Bay, United Kingdom few years ago. And I just started a new work (a church plant) in Monroe, Michigan; partnering with First Baptist church and the Philippine International Christian Church of Trenton, Michigan. To God be the glory! Amen

WEDNESDAY

THE HEART OF A PASTOR

(A Minister's Life from A to Z)

(Hebrews 13:7) "Remember them which have the rule over you, who have spoken unto you the word of God: whose faith follow, considering the end of their conversation."

A pastor could be a husband, a father, a friend and sometimes an enemy to others. A pastor could also be a brother, a manager and a broken hearted man. He is a man of God who is a blessing to others. A pastor is a counselor, a man of comfort, a man that you can count on, a considerate man and a man full of courage and firm in his conviction but sensitive in the leading of the Holy Spirit. He develops leaders, and a help to the disturbed, the discouraged and the depressed. A pastor is an encourager. He should be an eloquent speaker and an executor of the God given ministry. A pastor is a facilitator, one of the few good men, a fellow soldier, our fellowmen and a fellow servant. He is always on the "GO", and a great man of God. He should be a great communicator and a goal setter. A pastor's heart is in his home, in helping the needy and praying for the healing of the sick. A pastor's attitude should not be about "I" but about God and others. He is an imitator and he should be an inspiration to others and gives proper instructions for the kingdom. It is required for a pastor to be knowledgeable, to know what is best for his church, for his people and for the honor and glory of the King of kings. A pastor's love should be in his Lord. His life must be dedicated for the lost souls and he should be in line with what God wants for him to do as God's minister. He must remember that he is a man of God and a minister of the gospel of the Lord Jesus Christ. He carries the mark of the Lord Jesus Christ. He must be a minister with honor and humility. "17- Obey them that have the rule over you, and submit yourselves: for they watch for your souls, as they that must give account, that they may do it with joy, and not with grief: for that is unprofitable for you. 18- Pray for us: for we trust we have a good conscience, in all things willing to live honestly." (Hebrews

13:17- 18) A pastor is always neutral in his dealings with his people. He should not think or say; "It could never be done" neither be a man with negative aspects in life. He is willing to offer his best for the Master's use and he is a man who is open to new ideas. A man of God who perseveres…, he keeps on pressing on… He is a man who desires to please his Lord. He is a servant of God who never questions the Word of God, the will of God and the works of God. A man of God who always quotes the Word of God in all that he does. He learned to be quite. He resists the devil and that which is evil. He help restores those who have fallen in God's grace. He has a heart for revival, for regeneration of the lost world. He shows compassion, he depend on the Lord his God in everything. His success is because of what God did in him and through him. He trust the Lord, teaches the truth, he is truthful and faithful to God. He is not afraid to take the step of faith as the team leader. Unity is his passion and desire. He gives his undivided attention for the sake of Christ. He uses his talents, treasures and time for the Lord. Victory is on his side. He is a visionary and he values life, his family and spiritual things. Winning for God and working for God is his focus. Worldly pleasure is not on his list and he is willing to wait on God's time. Wine, womanizing, worldly wealth and wickedness are out of his line. A pastor should live in love, integrity and with dignity in his public life; it is also required of him to live a holy life and in righteousness in private. X-rated movies, x-rated magazines, x- rated - shows and any x-rated materials on the internet are something that he avoids. He has a heart for the young people, young at hearts and he yearns to love every individual. His yoke is the Lord's yoke. And his years are full of wisdom. A pastor must not waste his time in the service of the King. He must learn to trust God even in a zigzag road or in a rough road. He tried to be zealous in his relationship with God and man. And as a pastor, he is marching to Zion. In God's grace and by God's grace: Your pastor will serve you in spite of financial difficulties. He will love you and preach God's Word in spite of negative remarks of his people. He will be there for you in spite of your weakness, failure, unfaithfulness to God and in the church. He needs your prayer, your financial support, your understanding when things are not going well in your church. And most of all- he's like you with feelings and emotion. He has spiritual downfall, failures, and he is hurting. He is a needy person and he is going through tough times like you do. He needs God's grace, God's mercy and he needs YOU! Respect him like a soldier or a general in the army of God. "Salute all them that have the rule over you, and all the saints. They of Italy salute you." (Hebrews 13:24) "20- Now the God of peace, that brought again from the dead our Lord Jesus, that great shepherd of the sheep, through the blood of the everlasting covenant, 21- Make you perfect in every good work to do his will, working in you that which is well pleasing in his sight, through Jesus Christ; to whom be glory forever and ever. Amen." (Hebrews 13:20-21)

THURSDAY

GOD IS FAITHFUL IN KEEPING HIS CHILDREN IN HIS HANDS

(II Peter 2:9) "The Lord is not slack concerning his promise, as some men count slackness; but is longsuffering to us-ward, not willing that any should perish, but that all should come to repentance."

Here in Michigan, there's a car insurance company that has an ads which says, "… you're in good hands." In my own observation, it speaks of security and their assurance to their consumer that if you're with them or sign in to them; you will be safe and secured. But it's just about your car insurance which is really just about money and coverage. In the Bible, Paul was talking about our relationship with the Lord Jesus Christ and eternal life that cannot be broken up by anybody and anything at anytime and anywhere and by any circumstances in life. He wrote; "8- Who shall also confirm you unto the end, that ye may be blameless in the day of our Lord Jesus Christ. 9- God is faithful, by whom ye were called unto the fellowship of his Son Jesus Christ our Lord." (I Corinthians 1:8- 9) Our whole being is in the hands of God the Father and in the Lord Jesus Christ in which I believe is sealed by the Holy Spirit of God until the day of redemption. It means until that day when we see Him face to face. What a glory that will be. "23- And the very God of peace sanctify you wholly; and I pray God your whole spirit and soul and body be preserved blameless unto the coming of our Lord Jesus Christ. 24- Faithful is he that calleth you, who also will do it." (I Thessalonians 5:23- 24) You have heard His voice when you responded to His call for you to come to Him and follow Him for your salvation. If you did that, you are therefore with no doubt the son of the living God. What comes along with that is the promised of eternal life in heaven that cannot be taken away from you by sin, Satan and the world system. "27- My sheep hear my voice, and I know them, and they follow me: 28- And I give unto them eternal life; and they shall never perish, neither shall any man pluck them out of my hand. 29- My Father, which gave them me, is greater

than all; and no man is able to pluck them out of my Father's hand."
(John 10:27- 29)

God will remain faithful even if we will turn our back from
Him. He will not take the salvation away from anyone who sins
or was lacking in some ways. He is faithful to His promises and
the promised of eternal life in heaven and it's not based on our
performance and attitude, but was based on the cross of Calvary. He
paid it all and can't be taken back... It's not like a mortgage where
you have foreclosure and the bank could take your property or take
control of your business if you don't get to pay them... When I took
EJ my youngest son to a haunted house at the Universal Studio in
Florida; EJ was so scared and he was yelling and was about to cry.
I did not expect him to be so afraid because it was not that scary
outside. But every time EJ could feel my hands and when I'm by
his side; he felt safe and strong, especially when I assured him that
I will be with him. We have a greater promise from the Lord our
God who will always be there for us. Apostle Paul assured us...
"38- For I am persuaded, that neither death, nor life, nor angels,
nor principalities, nor powers, nor things present, nor things to
come, 39- Nor height, nor depth, nor any other creature, shall be
able to separate us from the love of God, which is in Christ Jesus
our Lord." (Romans 8:38- 39)

FRIDAY
THE DANGER OF LOSING OUR TEARS FOR THE LOST SOULS,
PRAYER AND SERVICE TO GOD

(Acts 6:2; 4) "2- Then the twelve called the multitude of the disciples unto them, and said, It is not reason that we should leave the word of God, and serve tables. 4- But we will give ourselves continually to prayer, and to the ministry of the word."

When was the last time we cried out to God for the ministry, for our church and for the work of the Lord in your community? When was the last time we cried out to God for the missionaries who serves the Lord in the ministry of the mission organizations on the other side of the globe? Many Christians and churches have lost that desire already; "4- But we will give ourselves continually to prayer, and to the ministry of the word." Picture in your mind the way King David prayed to God in the book of "I am weary of my crying: my throat is dried: mine eyes fail while I wait for my God." (Psalm 69:3) It's so unfortunate that many Christians and churches have lost the fire in their service and prayer life to God. We should at least search our heart if we are still walking with God both in our service and prayer life. "Search me, O God, and know my heart: try me, and know my thoughts:" (Psalm 139: 23) Paul gave us this great encouragement as we serve the King of kings. "Therefore, my beloved brethren, be ye steadfast, unmoveable, always abounding in the work of the Lord, forasmuch as ye know that your labour is not in vain in the Lord." (I Corinthians 15:58) In (Luke 13: 34-35) "34- O Jerusalem, Jerusalem, which killest the prophets, and stonest them that are sent unto thee; how often would I have gathered thy children together, as a hen doth gather her brood under her wings, and ye would not! 35- Behold, your house is left unto you desolate: and verily I say unto you, Ye shall not see me, until the time come when ye shall say, Blessed is he that cometh in the name of the Lord." I was sharing this little wisdom that I got from observing the churches in North America which could also be happening in many parts of the world.

I believe that in the United Kingdom, some churches are dying too. I was telling my friend that the reasons why some of the pastors could stay longer in their dying church, because they get used to it. They get used preaching to the same crowds. And when they were in the peak of their ministry and they don't feel the peace, joy and the passion to pastor in the same church, they stayed; thus they lost it. The other common problem is a little bit scary. It's when they don't feel the Lord's presence and they don't feel God is working in them and through them already and yet- they stayed! Jesus shed tears for Jerusalem as well as for every lost soul. He cried for those who have no hope, for the unsaved, for every individual who rejected Him as their Lord and Savior. Have you ever looked at your love ones right in their eyes with love, knowing that when this life will come to an end (God forbid) or when He comes back for His saints, they will not make it to heaven? It's one of the reasons why we must witness or have passion for the lost. We need to cry out to God for their salvation and we need to do something so they can hear the good news of salvation. In every sponsored concert of music prescription; we made sure that the gospel is shared and we extend an invitation for salvation. I hope and pray that pastors, artists, evangelists and the motivational speaker will do the same. That should be our main purpose and focus. Notice the passion of Apostle Paul in (Acts 20:24) "But none of these things move me, neither count I my life dear unto myself, so that I might finish my course with joy, and the ministry, which I have received of the Lord Jesus, to testify the gospel of the grace of God."

SATURDAY

IN TRIALS AND TEMPTATIONS, WE CAN TRIUMP IN GOD'S MERCY AND HIS FAITHFULNESS

(I Peter 4:13- 15) "13- But rejoice, inasmuch as ye are partakers of Christ's sufferings; that, when his glory shall be revealed, ye may be glad also with exceeding joy. 14- If ye be reproached for the name of Christ, happy are ye; for the spirit of glory and of God resteth upon you: on their part he is evil spoken of, but on your part he is glorified. 15- But let none of you suffer as a murderer, or as a thief, or as an evildoer, or as a busybody in other men's matters."

We all went through temptations and we will go through to a lot more while we're living and as long as we are here on earth. It means that temptation is part of the cycle of the Christian life. Paul warned us of not tempting the Lord Jesus Christ. "9- Neither let us tempt Christ, as some of them also tempted, and were destroyed of serpents. 10- Neither murmur ye, as some of them also murmured, and were destroyed of the destroyer. 11- Now all these things happened unto them for ensamples: and they are written for our admonition, upon whom the ends of the world are come. 12- Wherefore let him that thinketh he standeth take heed lest he fall. 13-There hath no temptation taken you but such as is common to man: but God is faithful, who will not suffer you to be tempted above that ye are able; but will with the temptation also make a way to escape, that ye may be able to bear it." (I Corinthians 10:9- 13) So temptation could be from us to God. It means that we should not put God to the test, lest we suffer the consequences of our sins as the Israelites did when they cling upon their lusts. (Exodus chapter 32)

"The Lord knoweth how to deliver the godly out of temptations, and to reserve the unjust unto the day of judgment to be punished:" (II Peter 2:9) The Lord promised us of deliverance according to Peter, but you have to live a godly life. He said, "The Lord knoweth how to deliver the godly out of temptations..." We need to be strong in the faith because Satan, our enemy is not taking a "time out" in his effort to deceive and destroy both Christians and his very own. Sometimes, Satan would start from a cookie in a cookie jar. He starts small to destroy big people, huge ministries and large amount of damages both in physical, financial, moral, emotional and spiritual life of a man or a woman. We know that prayer and the Word of God are our weapons against the wiles of the devil. We must use it to resist the enemy.

(I Peter 4:19) "Wherefore let them that suffer according to the will of God commit the keeping of their souls to him in well doing, as unto a faithful Creator."

SUNDAY
THE LORD IS FAITHFUL IN KEEPING HIS PROMISES TO HIS FRIENDS AND ENEMIES

(Revelation 2:9- 10) "9- I know thy works, and tribulation, and poverty, (but thou art rich) and I know the blasphemy of them which say they are Jews, and are not, but are the synagogue of Satan. 10- Fear none of those things which thou shalt suffer: behold, the devil shall cast some of you into prison, that ye may be tried; and ye shall have tribulation ten days: be thou faithful unto death, and I will give thee a crown of life."

Will it be possible for a Holy God to make some promises to His enemies? And what kind of promise or promises would He make to His enemies? First, we must remember that we are serving a true, Holy, Righteous and Just God. Secondly, we have to know what kind of promised does God have in stored for His enemies. I believe that God has promised them death, judgment and eternal punishment in hell. Notice what happened to Ahab- "And the word of the LORD came to Elijah the Tishbite, saying, 18- Arise, go down to meet Ahab king of Israel, which is in Samaria: behold, he is in the vineyard of Naboth, whither he is gone down to possess it. 19- And thou shalt speak unto him, saying, Thus saith the LORD, Hast thou killed, and also taken possession? And thou shalt speak unto him, saying, Thus saith the LORD, In the place where dogs licked the blood of Naboth shall dogs lick thy blood, even thine." (I Kings 21:17- 19) And compare (I Kings 22:34- 37) "34- And a certain man drew a bow at a venture, and smote the king of Israel between the joints of the harness: wherefore he said unto the driver of his chariot, Turn thine hand, and carry me out of the host; for I am wounded. 35- And the battle increased that day: and the king was stayed up in his chariot against the Syrians, and died at even: and the blood ran out of the wound into the midst of the chariot. 36-And there went a proclamation throughout the host about the going down of the sun, saying, Every man to his city, and every man to his own country. 37-So the king died, and was brought to

Samaria; and they buried the king in Samaria. 38- And one washed the chariot in the pool of Samaria; and the dogs licked up his blood; and they washed his armour; according unto the word of the LORD which he spake."

To Satan will be judge and cast down into hell and the bottomless pit. God promised us of the positive and good things in life, but He promised His enemies of the bad, negative and the coming wrath. To those who were called the children of disobedient and also to the father of lies- Satan and his angels. "7- And there was war in heaven: Michael and his angels fought against the dragon; and the dragon fought and his angels, 8- And prevailed not; neither was their place found any more in heaven. 9- And the great dragon was cast out, that old serpent, called the Devil, and Satan, which deceiveth the whole world: he was cast out into the earth, and his angels were cast out with him. 10- And I heard a loud voice saying in heaven, Now is come salvation, and strength, and the kingdom of our God, and the power of his Christ: for the accuser of our brethren is cast down, which accused them before our God day and night. 11- And they overcame him by the blood of the Lamb, and by the word of their testimony; and they loved not their lives unto the death. 12- Therefore rejoice, ye heavens, and ye that dwell in them. Woe to the inhabiters of the earth and of the sea! for the devil is come down unto you, having great wrath, because he knoweth that he hath but a short time." (Revelation 12:7- 12)

MONDAY

DO YOU WANT WEALTH, PRESTIGE, INTEGRITY OR GOD?

(Mark 8:35- 37) "35- For whosoever will save his life shall lose it; but whosoever shall lose his life for my sake and the gospel's, the same shall save it. 36- For what shall it profit a man, if he shall gain the whole world, and lose his own soul? 37- Or what shall a man give in exchange for his soul?"

This is a very simple question that many people could not answer without taking a pause. "Do you want wealth, prestige, integrity or God?" May we all could say; "I can't afford to trade my soul to wealth and worldly things or any worldly pleasures. And I will not ride on my personal conviction if it's against the Word of God." May the lost world will stand for the salvation of their soul even if it will cost them their worldly pleasure and wealth. May the children of God will stand and serve the Lord with integrity and the fear of God. May the believers of this present times will stand for what is right and pleasing to the Lord. May all those who comes behind us could say; "It was indeed a life that was pleasing to God and a life that was lived with dignity and integrity." I desire to live a life that may not be moved and not be deceived by money, by position, by people and prosperity. At the end of the day, may we all could say; "I have fought a good fight, I have finished my course, I have kept the faith:" (II Timothy 4:7). One of the questions for every believer in every generation would be: "Who do you serve? Or "Would you trade the Lord your God for money or wealth?" "Then there passed by Midianites merchantmen; and they drew and lifted up Joseph out of the pit, and sold Joseph to the Ishmeelites for twenty pieces of silver: and they brought Joseph into Egypt." (Genesis 37:28) It was his own brothers who betrayed him. Joseph's brothers were supposed to help him but it turned out to be the other way around. Joseph's own blood was the one who sold him as a slave. In (Matthew 26:15-16) "And said unto them, What will ye give me, and I will deliver him unto you? And they covenanted with him for thirty pieces of silver." Notice the phrase, "Judas was looking for the opportunity to betray the Lord." Do we look for the opportunity to serve God or to deny God for money or friends? Joseph was sold by his brother for 20 pieces of silver and Jesus was sold for thirty pieces of silver. We may actually have trade him for money, for fame, for position or possessions. "But they that will be rich fall into temptation and a snare, and into many foolish and hurtful lusts, which drown men in destruction and perdition. 10- For the love of money is the root of all evil: which while some coveted after, they have erred from the faith, and pierced themselves through with many sorrows." (I Timothy 6:9- 10) It's not Biblical to put money as your first priority instead of God. Some Christians sold him to friends by not letting them know that they're Christians. They trade Jesus for shame. They denied Him because they're ashamed of Him. They trade Jesus in some ways. This was Peter's attitude when he was confronted that he was Jesus' disciple and he denied Him. The Lord Jesus Christ is the Son of God and the true Messiah. You will either trust Him or deny Him as your Lord, Savior and King. It's so easy to get distracted with the world's pleasures, power, possessions and prosperity. May those will not stand in the way, in your worship and service for the Lord. Jesus said; "But seek ye first the kingdom of God, and his righteousness; and all these things shall be added unto you." (Matthew 6:33)

Mi Daily Devotion on the internet. Page views by countries: United States of America, Philippines, United Kingdom, Singapore, Canada, Israel, Kuwait, Denmark, Australia, Saudi Arabia, Colombia, United Arab Emirates, Germany, India, China, South Korea, Japan, Russia and many other countries. God's Word reaches unto the uttermost parts of the world from my dining table or from my small bedroom which serves to be an office. This is just from the said web page not including emails, Facebook and other web sites. Praise God!

THANKS TO:

Cyclopedia of Illustrations that was compiled by Robert Scott and William C. Stiles:
(CYCLOPEDIA OF ILLUSTRATIONS For Public Speakers, Funk and Wagnalls Company, New York and London 1911)

Faith, Prayer and Tract League
2627 Elmridge Drive Nw, Grand Rapids, MI

Felicidad T. E. Sagalongos. (Diksyunaryong Ingles- Filipino, Filipino- Ingles).

Holy Bible - KJV

Merriam-Webster Dictionary, Internet

International Community Christian Church
4049 Longmeadow Drive
Trenton, Michigan
48183

Philippine Census Office

Reverend and Mrs. Dennis Casaje
Wilshire Baptist Church- Wilshire, Los Angeles California

The Bible Collection, Matthew Henry

Reverend and Mrs. Jundy Bautista

Music Prescription
"The Cure of Music"
www.musicprescription.com

Eliel Lyn S.
www.facebook.com/eliellyn
You Tube @ Eliellyn3

www.nimh.nih.gov.

The Hymnal for Worship and Celebration
"There is Power in the Blood"
Lewis E. Jones

ABOUT THE AUTHOR

Reverend Ely Roque Sagansay was born in Bacolod City, Philippines. He grew up in a Christian home and four (4) of his siblings are in the pastorate. He is a graduate of International Baptist Theological College of Mandaluyong, Metro Manila, Philippines. He's been a pastor for 3 decades. He came to know the Lord Jesus Christ April of 1982. Pastor Ely is a teacher, a radio host and was a professor and administrator of International Baptist Theological College extension school in Subic, Zambales. He has served as director of music at the Greater Detroit Baptist Association of the Southern Baptist Convention (SBC). He is currently the pastor of International Community Christian Church in Trenton, Michigan; the church he started with the Southern Baptist Convention. Pastor Ely is the author of Mi Daily Devotion and the founder and owner of the devotional site on the internet at www.westbowpress.com/midailydevotion www.facebook.com/midailydevotion and http://www.midailydevotion.blogspot.com

Pastor Ely is married to former Bermilin Dumala from the Southern part of the Philippines. They were blessed by the Lord with four (4) children; Eliezer, Ely JR, Eliel Lyn and Elmer John (EJ). All of them are serving the Lord in the music ministry of his church. Pastor Ely Sagansay is very passionate about missions and he loves missionaries. He is a man of God and a man for God and for His glory.

ENDORSEMENT

Mi Daily Devotion by Reverend Ely Roque Sagansay is not just a devotional book; this is the blessing of his devotion to our GREAT GOD AND SAVIOR JESUS CHRIST. As you read through this inspiring devotional; read it thoughtfully, meditating and inquisitively to discover the overwhelming goodness, grace and plan of God in your life. The knowledge and the wisdom that you will learn from Mi Daily Devotion will lead you to a changed life. The book will lead you to a spiritual journey that will allow you to experience the hand of our loving God. You are a great blessing pastor Ely. Your faith and passion is contagiously good. God indeed is glorified in your life.

Reverend Jundy Bautista
Married to Joy Tarectecan Bautista
Pastor of Christian Church of Jersey City

Mi Daily Devotion (Second Edition) is sponsored by
Music Prescription.
www.musicprescription.com

Mi Daily Devotion is a Bible centered and God centered devotional. Discover God's grace, get closer to God and grow in the knowledge of the Lord Jesus Christ.